The Creative Process in the Individual

The Creative Process in the Individual

by Thomas Troward

Wilder Publications, LLC.
PO Box 3005
Radford VA 24143-3005

ISBN 10: 1-60459-064-5
ISBN 13: 978-1-60459-064-7

First Edition

10 9 8 7 6 5 4 3 2 1

FOREWORD

In the present volume I have endeavored to set before the reader the conception of a sequence of creative action commencing with the formation of the globe and culminating in a vista of infinite possibilities attainable by every one who follows up the right line for their unfoldment.

I have endeavored to show that, starting with certain incontrovertible scientific facts, all these things logically follow, and that therefore, however far these speculations may carry us beyond our past experience, they nowhere break the thread of an intelligible connection of cause and effect.

I do not, however, offer the suggestions here put forward in any other light than that of purely speculative reasoning; nevertheless, no advance in any direction can be made except by speculative reasoning going back to the first principles of things which we do know and thence deducing the conditions under which the same principles might be carried further and made to produce results hitherto unknown. It is to this method of thought that we owe all the advantages of civilization from matches and post-offices to motor-cars and aeroplanes, and we may therefore be encouraged to hope such speculations as the present may not be without their ultimate value. Relying on the maxim that Principle is not bound by Precedent we should not limit our expectations of the future; and if our speculations lead us to the conclusion that we have reached a point where we are not only able, but also *required* , by the law of our own being, to take a more active part in our personal evolution than heretofore, this discovery will afford us a new outlook upon life and widen our horizon with fresh interests and brightening hopes.

If the thoughts here suggested should help any reader to clear some mental obstacles from his path the writer will feel that he has not written to no purpose. Only each reader must think out these suggestions for himself. No writer or lecturer can convey an idea *into* the minds of his audience. He can only put it before them, and what they will make of it depends entirely upon themselves—assimilation is a process which no one can carry out for us.

To the kindness of my readers on both sides of the Atlantic, and in Australia and New Zealand, I commend this little volume, not, indeed, without a deep sense of its many shortcomings, but at the same time encouraged by the generous indulgence extended to my previous books.

T.T.

June, 1910.

TABLE OF CONTENTS

The Starting-Point 8

The Self-Contemplation of Spirit 13

The Divine Ideal 20

The Manifestation of the Life Principle 25

The Personal Factor 30

The Standard of Personality 36

Race Thought and New Thought 39

The Dénouement of the Creative Process 42

Conclusion 56

The Divine Offering 60

Ourselves in the Divine Offering 65

I say no man has ever yet been half devout enough,
None has ever yet adored or worship'd half enough,
None has begun to think how divine he himself is, and
how certain the future is.
I say that the real and permanent grandeur of these States
must be their religion,
Otherwise there is no real and permanent grandeur. —Walt Whitman.

THE STARTING-POINT

It is an old saying that "Order is Heaven's First Law," and like many other old sayings it contains a much deeper philosophy than appears immediately on the surface. Getting things into a better order is the great secret of progress, and we are now able to fly through the air, not because the laws of Nature have altered, but because we have learnt to arrange things in the right order to produce this result—the things themselves had existed from the beginning of the world, but what was wanting was the introduction of a Personal Factor which, by an intelligent perception of the possibilities contained in the laws of Nature, should be able to bring into working reality ideas which previous generations would have laughed at as the absurd fancies of an unbalanced mind. The lesson to be learnt from the practical aviation of the present day is that of the triumph of principle over precedent, of the working out of an *idea* to its logical conclusions in spite of the accumulated testimony of all past experience to the contrary; and with such a notable example before us can we say that it is futile to enquire whether by the same method we may not unlock still more important secrets and gain some knowledge of the unseen causes which are at the back of external and visible conditions, and then by bringing these unseen causes into a better order make practical working realities of possibilities which at present seem but fantastic dreams? It is at least worth while taking a preliminary canter over the course, and this is all that this little volume professes to attempt; yet this may be sufficient to show the lay of the ground.

Now the first thing in any investigation is to have some idea of what you are looking for—to have at least some notion of the general direction in which to go—just as you would not go up a tree to find fish though you would for birds' eggs. Well, the general direction in which we all want to go is that of getting more out of Life than we have ever got out of it—we want to be more alive in ourselves and to get all sorts of improved conditions in our environment. However happily any of us may be circumstanced we can all conceive something still better, or at any rate we should like to make our present good permanent; and since we shall find as our studies advance that the prospect of increasing possibilities keeps opening out more and more widely before us, we may say that what we are in search of is the secret of getting more out of Life in a continually progressive degree. This means that what we are looking for is something personal, and that it is to be obtained by producing conditions which do not yet exist; in other words it is nothing less than the exercise of a certain creative power in the sphere of our own particular world. So, then, what we want is to introduce our own Personal Factor into the realm of unseen causes. This is a big thing, and if it is possible at all it must be by some sequence of cause and effect, and this sequence it is our object to discover. The law of Cause and Effect is one we can never get away from, but by carefully following it up we may find that it will lead us further than we had anticipated.

Now, the first thing to observe is that if *we* can succeed in finding out such a sequence of cause and effect as the one we are in search of, somebody else may find out the same creative secret also; and then, by the hypothesis of the case, we should both be armed with an infallible power, and if we wanted to employ this power against each other we should be landed in the "impasse" of a conflict between two powers each of which was irresistible. Consequently it follows that the first principle of this power must be Harmony. It cannot be antagonizing itself from different centers—in other words its operation in a simultaneous order at every point is the first necessity of its being. What we are in search of, then, is a sequence of cause and effect so universal in its nature as to include harmoniously all possible variations of individual expression. This primary necessity of the Law for which we are seeking should be carefully borne in mind, for it is obvious that any sequence which transgresses this primary essential must be contrary to the very nature of the Law itself, and consequently cannot be conducting us to the exercise of true creative power.

What we are seeking, therefore, is to discover how to arrange things in such an order as to set in motion a train of causation that will harmonize our own conditions without antagonizing the exercise of a like power by others. This therefore means that all individual exercise of this power is the particular application of a universal power which itself operates creatively on its own account independently of these individual applications; and the harmony between the various individual applications is brought about by all the individuals bringing their own particular action into line with this independent creative action of the original power. It is in fact another application of Euclid's axiom that things which are equal to the same thing are equal to one another; so that though I may not know for what purpose some one may be using this creative power in Pekin, I do know that if he and I both realize its true nature, we cannot by any possibility be working in opposition to one another. For these reasons, having now some general idea of what it is we are in search of, we may commence our investigation by considering this common factor which must be at the back of all individual exercise of creative power, that is to say, the Generic working of the Universal Creative Principle.

That such a Universal Creative Principle is at work we at once realize from the existence of the world around us with all its inhabitants, and the inter-relation of all parts of the cosmic system shows its underlying Unity—thus the animal kingdom depends on the vegetable, the vegetable kingdom on the mineral, the mineral or globe of the earth on its relation to the rest of the solar system, and possibly our solar system is related by a similar law to the distribution of other suns with their attendant planets throughout space. Our first glance therefore shows us that the All-originating Power must be in essence Unity and in manifestation

Multiplicity, and that it manifests as Life and Beauty through the unerring adaptation of means to ends—that is so far as its cosmic manifestation of ends goes: what we want to do is to carry this manifestation still further by operation from an individual standpoint. To do this is precisely our place in the Order of Creation, but we must defer the question why we hold this place till later on.

One of the earliest discoveries we all make is the existence of Matter. The bruised shins of our childhood convince us of its solidity, so now comes the question, Why does Matter exist? The answer is that if the form were not expressed in solid substance, things would be perpetually flowing into each other so that no identity could be maintained for a single moment. To this it might be replied that a condition of matter is conceivable in which, though in itself a plastic substance, in a fluent state, it might yet by the operation of will be held in any particular forms desired. The idea of such a condition of matter is no doubt conceivable, and when the fluent matter was thus held in particular forms you would have concrete matter just as we know it now, only with this difference, that it would return to its fluent state as soon as the supporting will was withdrawn. Now, as we shall see later on, this is precisely what matter really is, only the will which holds it together in concrete form is not individual but cosmic.

In itself the Essence of Matter is precisely the fluent substance we have imagined, and as we shall see later on the knowledge of this fact, when realized in its proper order, is the basis of the legitimate control of mind over matter. But a world in which every individual possessed the power of concreting or fluxing matter at his own sweet will irrespective of any universal coordinating principle is altogether inconceivable—the conflict of wills would prevent such a world remaining in existence. On the other hand, if we conceive of a number of individuals each possessing this power and all employing it on the lines of a common cosmic unity, then the result would be precisely the same stable condition of matter with which we are familiar—this would be a necessity of fact for the masses who did not possess this power, and a necessity of principle for the few who did. So under these circumstances the same stable conditions of Nature would prevail as at present, varied only when the initiated ones perceived that the order of evolution would be furthered, and not hindered, by calling into action the higher laws. Such occasions would be of rare occurrence, and then the departure from the ordinary law would be regarded by the multitude as a miracle. Also we may be quite sure that no one who had attained this knowledge in the legitimate order would ever perform a "miracle" for his own personal aggrandizement or for the purpose of merely astonishing the beholders—to do so would be contrary to the first principle of the higher teaching which is that of profound reverence for the Unity of the All-originating Principle. The conception, therefore, of such a power over matter being possessed by certain individuals is in no way opposed to our ordinary recognition of concrete matter, and so we need not at present trouble ourselves to consider these exceptions.

Another theory is that matter has no existence at all but is merely an illusion projected by our own minds. If so, then how is it that we all project identically similar images? On the supposition that each mind is independently projecting its own conception of matter a lady who goes to be fitted might be seen by her dressmaker as a cow. Generations of people have seen the Great Pyramid on the same spot; but on the supposition that each individual is projecting his own material world in entire independence of all other individuals there is no reason why any two persons should ever see the same thing in the same place. On the supposition of such an independent action by each separate mind, without any common factor binding them all to one particular mode of recognition, no intercourse between individuals would be possible—then, without the consciousness of relation to other individuals the consciousness of our own individuality would be lost, and so we should cease to have any conscious existence at all. If on the other hand we grant that there is, above the individual minds, a great Cosmic Mind which imposes upon them the necessity of all seeing the same image of Matter, then that image is not a projection of the individual minds but of the Cosmic Mind; and since the individual minds are themselves similar projections of the Cosmic Mind, matter is for them just as much a reality as their own existence. I doubt not that material substance is thus projected by the all-embracing Divine Mind; but so also are our own minds projected by it, and therefore the relation between them and matter is a real relation and not a merely fictitious one.

I particularly wish the student to be clear on this point, that where two factors are projected from a common source their relation to each other becomes an absolute fact in respect of the factors themselves, notwithstanding that the power of changing that relation by substituting a different projection must necessarily always continue to reside in the originating source. To take a simple arithmetical example—by my power of mental projection working through my eyes and fingers I write 4 X 2. Here I have established a certain numerical relation which can only produce eight as its result. Again, I have power to change the factors and write 4 X 3, in which case 12 is the only possible result, and so on. Working in this way calculation becomes possible. But if every time I wrote 4 that figure possessed an independent power of setting down a different number by which to multiply itself, what would be the result? The first 4 I wrote might set down 3 as its multiplier, and the next might set down 7, and so on. Or if I want to make a box of a certain size and cut lengths of plank accordingly, if each length could capriciously change its width at a moment's notice, how could I ever make the box? I myself may change the shape and size of my box by establishing new relations between the bits of wood, but for the pieces of wood themselves the proportions determined by my mind must remain fixed quantities, otherwise no construction could take place.

This is a very rough analogy, but it may be sufficient to show that for a cosmos to exist at all it is absolutely necessary that there should be a Cosmic Mind binding all individual minds to certain *generic* unities of action, and so producing all things as realities and nothing as illusion. The importance of this conclusion will become more apparent as we advance in our studies.

We have now got at some reason why concrete material form is a necessity of the Creative Process. Without it the perfect Self-recognition of Spirit from the Individual standpoint, which we shall presently find is the means by which the Creative Process is to be carried forward, would be impossible; and therefore, so far from matter being an illusion, it is the necessary channel for the self-differentiation of Spirit and its Expression in multitudinous life and beauty. Matter is thus the necessary Polar Opposite to Spirit, and when we thus recognize it in its right order we shall find that there is no antagonism between the two, but that together they constitute one harmonious whole.

THE SELF-CONTEMPLATION OF SPIRIT

If we ask how the cosmos came into existence we shall find that ultimately we can only attribute it to the Self-Contemplation of Spirit. Let us start with the facts now known to modern physical science. All material things, including our own bodies, are composed of combinations of different chemical elements such as carbon, oxygen, nitrogen, &c. Chemistry recognizes in all about seventy of these elements each with its peculiar affinities; but the more advanced physical science of the present day finds that they are all composed of one and the same ultimate substance to which the name of Ether has been given, and that the difference between an atom of iron and an atom of oxygen results only from the difference in the number of etheric particles of which each is composed and the rate of their motion within the sphere of the atom, thus curiously coming back to the dictum of Pythagoras that the universe has its origin in Number and Motion. We may therefore say that our entire solar system together with every sort of material substance which it contains is made up of nothing but this one primary substance in various degrees of condensation.

Now the next step is to realize that this ether is everywhere. This is shown by the undulatory theory of light. Light is not a substance but is the effect produced on the eye by the impinging of the ripples of the ether upon the retina. These waves are excessively minute, ranging in length from 1-39,000th of an inch at the red end of the spectrum to 1-57,000th at the violet end. Next remember that these waves are not composed of advancing particles of the medium but pass onwards by the push which each particle in the line of motion gives to the particle next to it, and then you will see that if there were a break of one fifty-thousandth part of an inch in the connecting ether between our eye and any source of light we could not receive light from that source, for there would be nothing to continue the wave-motion across the gap. Consequently as soon as we see light from any source however distant, we know that there must be a continuous body of ether between us and it. Now astronomy shows us that we receive light from heavenly bodies so distant that, though it travels with the incredible speed of 186,000 miles per second, it takes more than two thousand years to reach us from some of them; and as such stars are in all quarters of the heavens we can only come to the conclusion that the primary substance or ether must be universally present.

This means that the raw material for the formation of solar systems is universally distributed throughout space; yet though we find that millions of suns stud the heavens, we also find vast interstellar spaces which show no sign of cosmic activity. Then something has been at work to start cosmic activity in certain areas while passing over others in which the raw material is equally available. What is this something? At first we might be inclined to attribute the development of cosmic energy to the etheric particles themselves, but a little consideration will show us that this is mathematically impossible in a medium which is equally distributed throughout space, for all its particles are in equilibrium and so no one particle possesses *per se* a greater power of originating motion than any other. Consequently the initial movement must be started by something which, though it works on and through the particles of the primary substance, is not those particles themselves. It is this "Something" which we mean when we speak of "Spirit."

Then since Spirit starts the condensation of the primary substance into concrete aggregation, and also does this in certain areas to the exclusion of others, we cannot avoid attributing to Spirit the power of Selection and of taking an Initiative on its own account.

Here, then, we find the *initial* Polarity of Universal Spirit and Universal Substance, each being the complementary of the other, and out of this relation all subsequent evolution proceeds. Being complementary means that each supplies what is wanting in the other, and that the two together thus make complete wholeness. Now this is just the case here. Spirit supplies Selection and Motion. Substance supplies something from which selection can be made and to which Motion can be imparted; so that it is a *sine qua non* for the Expression of Spirit.

Then comes the question, How did the Universal Substance get there? It cannot have made itself, for its only quality is inertia, therefore it must have come from some source having power to project it by some mode of action not of a material nature. Now the only mode of action not of a material nature is Thought, and therefore to Thought we must look for the origin of Substance. This places us at a point antecedent to the existence even of primary substance, and consequently the initial action must be that of the Originating Mind upon Itself, in other words, Self-contemplation.

At this primordial stage neither Time nor Space can be recognized, for both imply measurement of successive intervals, and in the primary movement of Mind upon itself the only consciousness must be that of Present Absolute Being, because no external points exist from which to measure extension either in time or space. Hence we must eliminate the ideas of time and space from our conception of Spirit's *initial* Self-contemplation.

This being so, Spirit's primary contemplation of itself as simply Being necessarily makes its presence universal and eternal, and consequently, paradoxical as it may seem, its independence of Time and Space makes it present throughout all Time and Space. It is the old esoteric maxim that the point expands to infinitude and that infinitude is concentrated in the point. We start, then, with Spirit contemplating itself simply as Being. But to realize your being you must have consciousness, and consciousness can only come by the recognition of your relation to something else. The something else may be an external fact or a mental image; but even in the latter case to conceive the image at all you must mentally stand back from it and look at it—something like the man who was run in by the police at

Gravesend for walking behind himself to see how his new coat fitted. It stands thus: if you are not conscious of something you are conscious of nothing, and if you are conscious of nothing, then you are unconscious, so that to be conscious at all you must have something to be conscious of.

This may seem like an extract from "Paddy's Philosophy," but it makes it clear that consciousness can only be attained by the recognition of something which is not the recognizing *ego* itself—in other words consciousness is the realization of some particular sort of *relation* between the cognizing subject and the cognized object; but I want to get away from academical terms into the speech of human beings, so let us take the illustration of a broom and its handle—the two together make a broom; that is one sort of relation; but take the same stick and put a rake-iron at the end of it and you have an altogether different implement. The stick remains the same, but the difference of what is put at the end of it makes the whole thing a broom or a rake. Now the thinking and feeling power is the stick, and the conception which it forms is the thing at the end of the stick, so that the quality of its consciousness will be determined by the ideas which it projects; but to be conscious at all it must project ideas of some sort.

Now of one thing we may be quite sure, that the Spirit of Life must *feel alive* . Then to feel alive it must be conscious, and to be conscious it must have something to be conscious of; therefore the contemplation of itself as standing related to something which is not its own originating self *in propria persona* is a necessity of the case; and consequently the Self-contemplation of Spirit can only proceed by its viewing itself as related to something standing out from itself, just as we must stand at a proper distance to see a picture—in fact the very word "existence" means "standing out." Thus things are called into existence or "outstandingness" by a power which itself does not stand out, and whose presence is therefore indicated by the word "subsistence."

The next thing is that since in the beginning there is nothing except Spirit, its primary feeling of aliveness must be that of being alive *all over* ; and to establish such a consciousness of its own universal livingness there must be the recognition of a corresponding *relation* equally extensive in character; and the only possible correspondence to fulfil this condition is therefore that of a universally distributed and plastic medium whose particles are all in perfect equilibrium, which is exactly the description of the Primary Substance or ether. We are thus philosophically led to the conclusion that Universal Substance must be projected by Universal Spirit as a necessary consequence of Spirit's own inherent feeling of Aliveness; and in this way we find that the great Primary Polarity of Being becomes established.

From this point onward we shall find the principle of Polarity in universal activity. It is that relation between opposites without which no external Motion would be possible, because there would be nowhere to move from, and nowhere to move to; and without which external Form would be impossible because there would be nothing to limit the diffusion of substance and bring it into shape. Polarity, or the interaction of Active and Passive, is therefore the basis of all *Evolution* .

This is a great fundamental truth when we get it in its right order; but all through the ages it has been a prolific source of error by getting it in its wrong order. And the wrong order consists in making Polarity the originating point of the Creative Process. What this misconception leads to we shall see later on; but since it is very widely accepted under various guises even at the present day it is well to be on our guard against it. Therefore I wish the student to see clearly that there is something which comes before that Polarity which gives rise to Evolution, and that this something is the original movement of Spirit *within itself* , of which we can best get an idea by calling it Self-contemplation.

Now this may seem an extremely abstract conception and one with which we have no practical concern. I fancy I can hear the reader saying "The Lord only knows how the world started, and it is His business and not mine," which would be perfectly true if this originating faculty were confined to the Cosmic Mind. But it is not, and the same action takes place in our own minds also, only with the difference that it is ultimately subject to that principle of Cosmic Unity of which I have already spoken. But, subject to that unifying principle, this same power of origination is in ourselves also, and our personal advance in evolution depends on our right use of it; and our use of it depends on our recognition that we ourselves give rise to the particular polarities which express themselves in our whole world of consciousness, whether within or without. For these reasons it is very important to realize that Evolution is not the same as Creation. It is the unfolding of potentialities involved in things already created, but not the calling into existence of what does not yet exist—*that* is Creation.

The order, therefore, which I wish the student to observe is, first the Self-contemplation of Spirit producing Polarity, and next Polarity producing Manifestation in Form—and also to realize that it is in this order his own mind operates as a subordinate center of creative energy. When the true place of Polarity is thus recognized, we shall find in it the explanation of all those relations of things which give rise to the whole world of phenomena; from which we may draw the practical inference that if we want to change the manifestation we must change the polarity, and to change the polarity we must get back to the Self-contemplation of Spirit. But in its proper place as the root-principle of all *secondary* causation, Polarity is one of those fundamental facts of which we must never lose sight. The term "Polarity" is adopted from electrical science. In the electric battery it is the connecting together of the opposite poles of zinc and copper that causes a current to flow from one to the other and so provides the energy that rings the bell. If the connection is broken there is no action. When you press the button you make the connection. The same process is repeated in respect of every sort of polarity throughout the universe. Circulation depends on polarity, and circulation is the *manifestation* of Life, which we may therefore say depends on the principle of polarity. In relation to ourselves we are concerned with two great polarities, the polarity of Soul and Body and the polarity of Soul and Spirit; and it is in order that he may more clearly realize their working that I want the student to have some preliminary idea of Polarity as a general principle.

The conception of the Creative Order may therefore be generalized as follows. The Spirit wants to enjoy the reality of its own Life—not merely to vegetate, but to enjoy giving—and therefore by Self-contemplation it projects a polar opposite, or complementary, calculated to give rise to the particular sort of *relation* out of which the enjoyment of a certain mode of self-consciousness will necessarily spring. Let this sentence be well pondered over until the full extent of its significance is grasped, for it is the key to the whole matter Very well, then: Spirit wants to Enjoy Life, and so, by thinking of itself as *having* the enjoyment which it wishes, it produces the conditions which, by their re-action upon itself, give rise to the reality of the sort of enjoyment contemplated. In more scientific language an opposite polarity is induced, giving rise to a current which stimulates a particular mode of sensation, which sensation in turn becomes a fresh starting-point for still further action; and in this way each successive stage becomes the stepping-stone to a still higher degree of sensation—that is, to a Fuller Enjoyment of Life.

Such a conception as this presents us with a Progressive Series to which it is impossible to assign any limit. That the progression must be limitless is clear from the fact that there is never any change in the method. At each successive stage the Creating Power is the Self-consciousness of the Spirit, as realized at that stage, still reaching forward for yet further Enjoyment of Life, and so always keeping on repeating the *one* Creative Process at an ever-rising level; and since these are the sole working conditions, the progress is one which logically admits of no finality. And this is where the importance of realizing the Singleness of the Originating Power comes in, for with a Duality each member would limit the other; in fact, Duality as the Originating Power is inconceivable, for, once more to quote "Paddy's Philosophy," "finality would be reached before anything was begun."

This Creative Process, therefore, can only be conceived of as limitless, while at the same time strictly progressive, that is, proceeding stage by stage, each stage being necessary as a preparation for the one that is to follow. Let us then briefly sketch the stages by which things in our world have got as far as they have. The interest of the enquiry lies in the fact that if we can once get at the principle which is producing these results, we may discover some way of giving it personal application.

On the hypothesis of the Self-contemplation of Spirit being the originating power, we have found that a primary ether, or universal substance, is the necessary correspondence to Spirit's simple awareness of its own being. But though awareness of being is the necessary foundation for any further possibilities it is, so to say, not much to talk about. The foundation fact, of course, is to know that I Am; but immediately on this consciousness there follows the desire for Activity—I want to enjoy my I Am-ness by doing something with it. Translating these words into a state of consciousness in the Cosmic Mind they become a Law of Tendency leading to *localised* activity, and, looking only at our own world, this would mean the condensation of the universal etheric substance into the primary nebula which later on becomes our solar system, this being the correspondence to the Self-contemplation of Spirit as passing into specific activity instead of remaining absorbed in simple awareness of Being. Then this self-recognition would lead to the conception of still more specific activity having its appropriate polar opposite, or material correspondence, in the condensation of the nebula into a solar system.

Now at this stage Spirit's conception of itself is that of Activity, and consequently the material correspondence is Motion, as distinguished from the simple diffused ether which is the correspondence of mere awareness of Being, But what sort of motion? Is the material movement evolved at this stage bound to take any particular form? A little consideration will show us that it is. At this initial stage, the first awakening, so to say, of Spirit into activity, its consciousness can only be that of activity *absolute* ; that is, not as related to any other mode of activity because as yet there is none, but only as related to an all-embracing Being; so that the only possible conception of Activity at this stage is that of *Self-sustained* activity, not depending on any preceding mode of activity because there is none. The law of reciprocity therefore demands a similar self-sustained motion in the material correspondence, and mathematical considerations show that the only sort of motion which can sustain a self-supporting body moving *in vacuo* is a rotary motion bringing the body itself into a spherical form. Now this is exactly what we find at both extremes of the material world. At the big end the spheres of the planets rotating on their axes and revolving round the sun; and at the little end the spheres of the atoms consisting of particles which, modern science tells us, in like manner rotate round a common center at distances which are astronomical as compared with their own mass. Thus the two ultimate units of physical manifestation, the atom and the planet, both follow the same law of self-sustained motion which we have found that, on *a priori* grounds, they ought in order to express the primary activity of Spirit. And we may note in passing that this rotary, or *absolute*, motion is the combination of the only two possible *relative* modes of motion, namely, motion from a point and motion to it, that is to say centrifugal and centripetal motion; so that in rotary, or absolute, motion we find that both the polarities of motion are included, thus repeating on the purely mechanical side the primordial principle of the Unity including the Duality in itself.

But the Spirit wants something more than mechanical motion, something more alive than the preliminary Rota, and so the first step toward individualized consciousness meets us in plant life. Then on the principle that each successive stage affords the platform for a further outlook, plant life is followed by animal life, and this by the Human order in which the liberty of selecting its own conditions is immensely extended. In this way the Spirit's expression of itself has now reached the point where its polar complementary, or Reciprocal, manifests as Intellectual Man—thus constituting the Fourth great stage of Spirit's Self-recognition. But the Creative Process cannot stop here, for, as we have seen, its root in the Self-contemplation of Spirit renders it of necessity an Infinite Progression. So it is no use asking what is its ultimate, for it has no ultimate—its word is "Excelsior"—ever Life and "Life more Abundant." Therefore the question is not as to finality where there is none, but as to the next step in the progression. Four kingdoms we know: what is to be the Fifth? All along the line the progress has been in one direction, namely, toward the development of more perfect Individuality, and therefore on the principle of continuity we may reasonably infer that the next stage will take us still further in the same direction. We want something more perfect than we have yet reached, but our ideas as to what it should be are very various, not to say discordant, for one person's idea of better is another person's idea of worse. Therefore what we want to get at is some broad generalization of principle which will be in advance of our past experiences. This means that we must look for this principle in something that we have not yet experienced, and the only place where we can possibly find principles which have not yet manifested themselves is *in gremio Dei* —that is, in the innermost of the Originating Spirit, or as St. John calls it, "in the bosom of the Father." So we are logically brought to personal participation in the Divine Ideal as the only principle by which the advance into the next stage can possibly be made. Therefore we arrive at the question, What is the Divine Ideal like?

THE DIVINE IDEAL

What is the Divine Ideal? At first it might appear hopeless to attempt to answer such a question, but by adhering to a definite principle we shall find that it will open out, and lead us on, and show us things which we could not otherwise have seen—this is the nature of principle, and is what distinguishes it from mere rules which are only the application of principle under some particular set of conditions. We found two principles as essential in our conception of the Originating Spirit, namely its power of Selection and its power of Initiative; and we found a third principle as its only possible Motive, namely the Desire of the *living* for ever increasing Enjoyment of Life. Now with these three principles as the very essence of the All-originating Spirit to guide us, we shall, I think, be able to form some conception of that Divine Ideal which gives rise to the Fifth Stage of Manifestation of Spirit, upon which we should now be preparing to enter.

We have seen that the Spirit's Enjoyment of Life is necessarily a *reciprocal* —it must have a corresponding fact in manifestation to answer to it; otherwise by the inherent law of mind no consciousness, and consequently no enjoyment, could accrue; and therefore by the law of continuous progression the required Reciprocal should manifest as a being awakening to the consciousness of the principle by which he himself comes into existence.

Such an awakening cannot proceed from a comparison of one set of existing conditions with another, but only from the recognition of a Power which is independent of all conditions, that is to say, the absolute Self-dependence of the Spirit. A being thus awakened would be the proper correspondence of the Spirit's Enjoyment of Life at a stage not only above mechanical motion or physical vitality, but even above intellectual perception of existing phenomena, that is to say at the stage where the Spirit's Enjoyment consists in recognizing itself as the Source of all things. The position in the Absolute would be, so to speak, the awakening of Spirit to the recognition of its own Artistic Ability. I use the word "Artistic" as more nearly expressing an almost unstatable idea than any other I can think of, for the work of the artist approaches more closely to creation *ex nihilo* than any other form of human activity. The work of the artist is the expression of the self that the artist is, while that of the scientist is the comparison of facts which exist independently of his own personality. It is true that the realm of Art is not without its methods of analysis, but the analysis is that of the artist's own feeling and of the causes which give rise to it. These are found to contain in themselves certain principles which are fundamental to all Art, but these principles are the laws of the creative action of mind rather than those of the limitations of matter. Now if we may transfer this familiar analogy to our conception of the working of the All-Originating Mind we may picture it as the Great Artist giving visible expression to His feeling by a process which, though subject to no restriction from antecedent conditions, yet works by a Law which is inseparable from the Feeling itself—in fact the Law *is* the Feeling, and the Feeling *is* the Law, the Law of Perfect Creativeness.

Some such Self-contemplation as this is the only way in which we can conceive the next, or Fifth, stage of Spirit's Self-recognition as taking place. Having got as far as it has in the four previous stages, that is to the production of intellectual man as its correspondence, the next step in advance must be on the lines I have indicated—unless, indeed, there were a sudden and arbitrary breaking of the Law of Continuity, a supposition which the whole Creative Process up to now forbids us to entertain. Therefore we may picture the Fifth stage of the Self-contemplation of Spirit as its awakening to the recognition of its own Artistic Ability, its own absolute freedom of action and creative power—just as in studio parlance we say that an artist becomes "free of his palette." But by the always present Law of Reciprocity, through which alone self-consciousness can be attained, this Self-recognition of Spirit in the Absolute implies a corresponding objective fact in the world of the Relative; that is to say, the coming into manifestation of a being capable of realizing the Free Creative Artistry of the Spirit, and of recognizing the same principle in himself, while at the same time realizing also the *relation* between the Universal Manifesting Principle and its Individual Manifestation.

Such, it appears to me, must be the conception of the Divine Ideal embodied in the Fifth Stage of the progress of manifestation. But I would draw particular attention to the concluding words of the last paragraph, for if we miss the *relation* between the Universal Manifesting Principle and its Individual Manifestation, we have failed to realize the Principle altogether, whether in the Universal or in the Individual—it is just their interaction that makes each become what it does become—and in this further becoming consists the progression. This relation proceeds from the principle I pointed out in the opening chapter which makes it necessary for the Universal Spirit to be always harmonious with itself; and if this Unity is not recognized by the individual he cannot hold that position of Reciprocity to the Originating Spirit which will enable it to recognize itself as in the Enjoyment of Life at the higher level we are now contemplating—rather the feeling conveyed would be that of something antagonistic, producing the reverse of enjoyment, thus philosophically bringing out the point of the Scriptural injunction, "Grieve not the Spirit." Also the re-action upon the individual must necessarily give rise to a corresponding state of inharmony, though he may not be able to define his feeling of unrest or to account for it. But on the other hand if the grand harmony of the Originating Spirit within itself is duly regarded, then the individual mind affords a fresh center from which the Spirit contemplates itself in what I have ventured to call its Artistic Originality—a boundless potential of Creativeness, yet always regulated by its own inherent Law of Unity.

And this Law of the Spirit's Original Unity is a very simple one. It is the Spirit's necessary and basic conception of itself. A lie is a statement that something is, which is not. Then, since the Spirit's statement or conception of anything necessarily makes that thing exist, it is logically impossible for it to conceive a lie. Therefore the Spirit is Truth. Similarly disease and death are the negative of Life, and therefore the Spirit, as the Principle of Life, cannot embody disease or death in its Self-contemplation. In like manner also, since it is free to produce what it will, the Spirit cannot desire the presence of repugnant forms, and so one of its inherent Laws must be Beauty. In this threefold Law of Truth, Life, and Beauty, we find the whole underlying nature of the Spirit, and no action on the part of the individual can be at variance with the Originating Unity which does not contravert these fundamental principles.

This it will be seen leaves the individual absolutely unfettered except in the direction of breaking up the fundamental harmony on which he himself, as included in the general creation, is dependent. This certainly cannot be called limitation, and we are all free to follow the lines of our own individuality in every other direction; so that, although the recognition of our relation to the Originating Spirit safeguards us from injuring ourselves or others, it in no way restricts our liberty of action or narrows our field of development. Am I, then, trying to base my action upon a fundamental desire for the opening out of Truth, for the increasing of Livingness, and for the creating of Beauty? Have I got this as an ever present Law of Tendency at the back of my thought? If so, then this law will occupy precisely the same place in My Microcosm, or personal world, that it does in the Macrocosm, or great world, as a power which is in itself formless, but which by reason of its presence necessarily impresses its character upon all that the creative energy forms. On this basis the creative energy of the Universal Mind may be safely trusted to work through the specializing influence of our own thought[1] and we may adopt the maxim "trust your desires" because we know that they are the movement of the Universal in ourselves, and that being based upon our fundamental recognition of the Life, Love, and Beauty which the Spirit is, their unfoldments must carry these initial qualities with them all down the line, and thus, in however small a degree, becomes a portion of the working of the Spirit in its inherent creativeness.

This perpetual Creativeness of the Spirit is what we must never lose sight of, and that is why I want the student to grasp clearly the idea of the Spirit's Self-contemplation as the only possible root of the Creative Process. Not only at the first creation of the world, but at all times the plane of the innermost is that of Pure Spirit,[2] and therefore at this, the originating point, there is nothing else for Spirit to contemplate excepting itself; then this Self-contemplation produces corresponding manifestation, and since Self-contemplation or recognition of its own existence must necessarily go on continually, the corresponding creativeness must always be at work. If this fundamental idea be clearly grasped we shall see that incessant and progressive creativeness is the very essence and being of Spirit. This is what is meant by the Affirmativeness of the Spirit. It cannot *per se* act negatively, that is to say uncreatively, for by the very nature of its Self-recognition such a negative action would be impossible. Of course if *we* act negatively then, since the Spirit is always acting affirmatively, we are moving in the opposite direction to it; and consequently so long as we regard our own negative action as being affirmative, the Spirit's action must appear to us negative, and thus it is that all the negative conditions of the world have their root in negative or inverted thought: but the more we bring our thought into harmony with the Life, Love, and Beauty which the Spirit is, the less these inverted conditions will obtain, until at last they will be eliminated altogether. To accomplish this is our great object; for though the progress may be slow it will be steady if we proceed on a definite principle; and to lay hold of the true principle is the purpose of our studies. And the principle to lay hold of is the Ceaseless Creativeness of Spirit. This is what we mean when we speak of it as The Spirit of the Affirmative, and I would ask my readers to impress this term upon their minds. Once grant that the All-originating Spirit is thus the Spirit of the Pure Affirmative, and we shall find that this will lead us logically to results of the highest value.

If, then, we keep this Perpetual and Progressive Creativeness of the Spirit continually in mind we may rely upon its working as surely in ourselves as in that great cosmic forward movement which we speak of as Evolution. It is the same power of Evolution working within ourselves, only with this difference, that in proportion as we come to realize its nature we find ourselves able to facilitate its progress by offering more and more favorable conditions for its working. We do not add to the force of the Power, for we are products of it and so cannot generate what generates *us* ; but by providing suitable conditions we can more and more highly specialize it. This is the method of all the advance that has ever been made. We never create any force (*e.g.* electricity) but we provide special conditions under which the force manifests *itself* in a variety of useful and beautiful ways, unsuspected possibilities which lay hidden in the power until brought to light by the cooperation of the Personal Factor.

Now it is precisely the introduction[3] of this Personal Factor that concerns us, because to all eternity we can only recognize things from our own center of consciousness, whether in this world or in any other; therefore the practical question is how to specialize in our own case the *generic* Originating Life which, when we give it a name, we call "the Spirit." The method of doing this is perfectly logical when we once see that the principle involved is that of the Self-recognition of Spirit. We have traced the *modus operandi* of the Creative Process sufficiently far to see that the existence of the cosmos is the result of the Spirit's seeing itself *in* the cosmos, and if this be the law of the whole it must also be the law of the part. But there is this difference, that so long as the normal average relation of particles is maintained the whole continues to subsist, no matter what position any particular particle may go into, just as a fountain continues to exist no matter whether any particular drop of water is down in the basin or at the top of the jet. This is the *generic* action which keeps the race going as a whole. But the question is, What is going to become of ourselves? Then because the law of the whole is also the law of the part we may at once say that what is wanted is for the Spirit *to see itself in us* —in other words, to find in us the Reciprocal which, as we have seen, is necessary to its Enjoyment of a certain Quality of Consciousness. Now, the fundamental consciousness of the Spirit must be that of Self-sustaining Life, and for the full enjoyment of this consciousness there must be a corresponding *individual* consciousness reciprocating it; and on the part of the individual such a consciousness can only arise from the recognition that his own life is identical with that of the Spirit—not something sent forth to wander away by itself, but something included in and forming part of the Greater Life. Then by the very conditions of the case, such a contemplation on the part of the individual is nothing else than the Spirit contemplating itself from the standpoint of the individual consciousness, and thus fulfilling the Law of the Creative Process under such specialized conditions as must logically result in the perpetuation of the individual life. It is the Law of the Cosmic Creative Process transferred to the individual.

This, it seems to me, is the Divine Ideal: that of an Individuality which recognizes its Source, and recognizes also the method by which it springs from that Source, and which is therefore able to open up in itself a channel by which that Source can flow in uninterruptedly; with the result that from the moment of this recognition the individual lives directly from the Originating Life, as being himself *a special direct creation* , and not merely as being a member of a generic race. The individual who has reached this stage of recognition thus finds a principle of enduring life *within himself*; so then the next question is in what way this principle is likely to manifest itself.

THE MANIFESTATION OF THE LIFE PRINCIPLE

We must bear in mind that what we have now reached is a principle, or universal potential, only we have located it in the individual. But a principle, as such, is not manifestation. Manifestation is the growth proceeding *from* the principle, that is to say, some Form in which the principle becomes active. At the same time we must recollect that, though a form is necessary for manifestation, *the* form is not essential, for the same principle may manifest through various forms, just as electricity may work either through a lamp or a tram-car without in any way changing its inherent nature. In this way we are brought to the conclusion that the Life-principle must always provide itself with a body in which to function, though it does not follow that this body must always be of the same chemical constitution as the one we now possess. We might well imagine some distant planet where the chemical combinations with which we are familiar on earth did not obtain; but if the essential life-principle of any individual were transported thither, then by the Law of the Creative Process it would proceed to clothe itself with a material body drawn from the atmosphere and substance of that planet; and the personality thus produced would be quite at home there, for all his surroundings would be perfectly natural to him, however different the laws of Nature might be there from what we know here.

In such a conception as this we find the importance of the two leading principles to which I have drawn attention—first, the power of the Spirit to create *ex nihilo* , and secondly, the individual's recognition of the basic principle of Unity giving permanence and solidity to the frame of Nature. By the former the self-recognizing life-principle could produce any sort of body it chose; and by the latter it would be led to project one in harmony with the natural order of the particular planet, thus making all the facts of that order solid realities to the individual, and himself a solid and natural being to the other inhabitants of that world. But this would not do away with the individual's knowledge of how he got there; and so, supposing him to have realized his identity with the Universal Life-Principle sufficiently to consciously control the projection of his own body, he could at will disintegrate the body which accorded with the conditions of one planet and constitute one which accorded just as harmoniously with those of another, and could thus function on any number of planets as a perfectly natural being on each of them. He would in all respects resemble the other inhabitants with one all-important exception, that since he had attained to unity with his Creative Principle he would not be tied by the laws of matter as they were.

Any one who should attain to such a power could only do so by his realization of the all-embracing Unity of the Spirit as being the Foundation of all things; and this being the basis of his own extended powers he would be the last to controvert his own basic principle by employing his powers in such a way as to disturb the natural course of evolution in the world where he was. He might use them to help forward the evolution of others in that world, but certainly never to disturb it, for he would always act on the maxim that "Order is Heaven's First Law."

Our object, however, is not to transfer ourselves to other planets but to get the best out of this one; but we shall not get the best out of this one until we realize that the power which will enable us to do so is so absolutely universal and fundamental that its application in this world is precisely the same as in any other, and that is why I have stated it as a general proposition applicable to all worlds.

The principle being thus universal there is no reason why we should postpone its application till we find ourselves in another world, and the best place and time to begin are Here and Now. The starting point is not in time or locality, but in the mode of Thought; and if we realize that this Point of Origination is Spirit's power to produce something out of nothing, and that it does this in accordance with the natural order of substance of the particular world in which it is working, then the spiritual ego in ourselves, as proceeding direct from the Universal Spirit, should be able first, to so harmoniously combine the working of spiritual and physical laws in its own body as to keep it in perfect health, secondly to carry this process further and renew the body, thus eradicating the effects of old age, and thirdly to carry the process still further and perpetuate this renewed body as long as the individual might desire.

If the student shows this to one of his average acquaintances who has never given any thought to these things, his friend will undoubtedly exclaim "Tommy rot!" even if he does not use a stronger expletive. He will at once appeal to the past experience of all mankind, his argument being that what has not been in the past cannot be in the future; yet he does not apply the same argument to aeronautics and is quite oblivious of the fact that the Sacred Volume which he reverences contains promises of these very things. The really earnest student must never forget the maxim that "Principle is not bound by Precedent"—if it were we should still be primitive savages.

To use the Creative Process we must Affirm the Creative Power, that is to say, we must go back to the Beginning of the series and start with Pure Spirit, only remembering that this starting-point is now to be found *in ourselves*, for this is what distinguishes the individual Creative Process from the cosmic one. This is where the importance of realizing only *one* Originating Power instead of two interacting powers comes in, for it means that we do not derive our power from any existing polarity, but that we are going to establish polarities which will start secondary causation on the lines which we thus determine. This also is where the importance comes in of recognizing that the only possible originating movement of spirit must be Self-contemplation, for this shows us that we do not have to contemplate existing conditions but the Divine Ideal, and that this contemplation of the Divine Ideal of Man is the Self-contemplation of the Spirit from the standpoint of Human Individuality.

Then the question arises, if these principles are true, why are we not demonstrating them? Well, when our fundamental principle is obviously correct and yet we do not get the proper results, the only inference is that somewhere or other we have introduced something antagonistic to the fundamental principle, something not inherent in the principle itself and which therefore owes its presence to some action of our own. Now the error consists in the belief that the Creative Power is limited by the material in which it works. If this be assumed, then you have to calculate the resistances offered by the material; and since by the terms of the Creative Process these resistances do not really exist, you have no basis of calculation at all—in fact you have no means of knowing where you are, and everything is in confusion. This is why it is so important to remember that the Creative Process is the action of a Single Power, and that the interaction of two opposite polarities comes in at a later stage, and is not creative, but only distributive—that is to say, it localizes the Energy already proceeding from the Single Power. This is a fundamental truth which should never be lost sight of. So long, however, as we fail to see this truth we necessarily limit the Creative Power by the material it works in, and in practise we do this by referring to past experience as the only standard of judgment. We are measuring the Fifth Kingdom by the standard of the Fourth, as though we should say that an intellectual man, a being of the Fourth Kingdom, was to be limited by the conditions which obtain in the First or Mineral Kingdom—to use Scriptural language we are seeking the Living among the dead.

And moreover at the present time a new order of experience is beginning to open out to us, for well authenticated instances of the cure of disease by the invisible power of the Spirit are steadily increasing in number. The facts are now too patent to be denied—what we want is a better knowledge of the power which accounts for them. And if this beginning is now with us, by what reason can we limit it? The difference between the healing of disease and the renewal of the entire organism and the perpetuation of life is only a difference of degree and not of kind; so that the actual experience of increasing numbers shows the working of a principle to which we can logically set no limits.

If we get the steps of the Creative Process clearly into our minds we shall see why we have hitherto had such small results.

Spirit creates by Self-contemplation;
Therefore, What it contemplates itself
as being, that it becomes.
You are individualized Spirit;
Therefore, What you contemplate as
the Law of your being becomes the

Law of your being.

Hence, contemplate a Law of Death arising out of the Forces of the Material reacting against the Power of the Spirit and overcoming it, and you impress this mode of self-recognition upon Spirit in yourself. Of course you cannot alter its inherent nature, but you cause it to work under negative conditions and thus make it produce negative results so far as you yourself are concerned.

But reverse the process, and contemplate a Law of Life as inherent in the very Being of the Spirit, and therefore as inherent in spirit in yourself; and contemplate the forces of the Material as practically non-existent in the Creative Process, because they are products of it and not causes—look at things in this way and you will impress a corresponding conception upon the Spirit which, by the Law of Reciprocity, thus enters into Self-contemplation on *these* lines from the standpoint of your own individuality; and then by the nature of the Creative Process a corresponding externalization is bound to take place. Thus our initial question, How did anything come into existence at all, brings us to the recognition of a Law of Life which we may each specialize for ourselves; and in the degree to which we specialize it we shall find the Creative Principle at work within us building up a healthier and happier personality in mind, body, and circumstances.

Only we must learn to distinguish the vehicles of Spirit from Spirit itself, for the distinction has very important bearings. What distinguishes the vehicles from the Spirit is the Law of Growth. The Spirit is the Formless principle of Life, and the vehicle is a Form in which this principle functions. Now the vehicle is a projection by the Spirit of substance coordinate with the natural order of the plane on which the vehicle functions, and therefore requires to be built up comformably to that order. This building up is what we speak of as Growth; and since the principle which causes the growth is the individualized Spirit, the rate at which the growth will go on will depend on the amount of vitalizing energy the Spirit puts into it, and the amount of vitalizing energy will depend on the degree in which the individualized Spirit appreciates its own livingness, and finally the degree of this appreciation will depend on the quality of the individual's perception of the Great All-originating Spirit as reflecting itself in him and thus making his contemplation of It nothing else than the Creative Self-contemplation of the Spirit proceeding from an individual and personal center. We must therefore not omit the Law of Growth in the vehicle from our conception of the working of the Spirit. As a matter of fact the vehicle has nothing to say in the matter for it is simply a projection from the Spirit; but for this very reason its formation will be slow or rapid in exact proportion to the individual spirit's vitalizing conception. We could imagine a degree of vitalizing conception that would produce the corresponding form instantaneously, but at present we must allow for the weakness of our spiritual power—not as thinking it by any means incapable of accomplishing its object, but as being far slower in operation now than we hope to see it in the future—and so we must not allow ourselves to be discouraged, but must hold our thought knowing that it is doing its creative work, and that the corresponding growth is slowly but surely taking place—thus following the Divine precept that men ought always to pray and not to faint. Gradually as we gain experience on these new lines our confidence in the power of the Spirit will increase, and we shall be less inclined to argue from the negative side of things, and thus the hindrances to the inflow of the Originating Spirit will be more and more removed, and greater and greater results will be obtained.

If we would have our minds clear on this subject of Manifestation we should remember its threefold nature:—First the General Life-Principle, secondly the Localization of this principle in the Individual, and thirdly the Growth of the Vehicle as it is projected by the individualized spirit with more or less energy. It is a sequence of progressive condensation from the Undifferentiated Universal Spirit to the ultimate and outermost vehicle—a truth enshrined in the esoteric maxim that "Matter is Spirit at its lowest level."

The forms thus produced are in true accord with the general order of Nature on the particular plane where they occur, and are therefore perfectly different from forms temporarily consolidated out of material drawn from other living organisms. These latter phantasmal bodies are held together only by an act of concentrated volition, and can therefore only be maintained for a short time and with effort; while the body which the individualized spirit, or ego, builds for itself is produced by a perfectly natural process and does not require any effort to sustain it, since it is kept in touch with the whole system of the planet by the continuous and effortless action of the individual's sub-conscious mind.

This is where the action of sub-conscious mind as the builder of the body comes in. Sub-conscious mind acts in accordance with the aggregate of suggestion impressed upon it by the conscious mind, and if this suggestion is that of perfect harmony with the physical laws of the planet then a corresponding building by the sub-conscious mind will take place, a process which, so far from implying any effort, consists rather in a restful sense of unity with Nature.[4]

And if to this sense of union with the Soul of Nature, that Universal Sub-conscious Mind which holds in the cosmos the same place that the sub-conscious mind does in ourselves—if to this there be superadded a sense of union with the All-creating Spirit from which the Soul of Nature flows, then through the medium of the individual's sub-conscious mind such specialized effects can be produced in his body as to transcend our past experiences without in any way violating the order of the universe. The Old Law was the manifestation of the Principle of Life working under constricted conditions: the New Law is the manifestation of the same Principle working under expanding conditions. Thus it is that though God never changes we are said to "increase with the increase of God."

THE PERSONAL FACTOR

I have already pointed out that the presence of a single all-embracing Cosmic Mind is an absolute necessity for the existence of any creation whatever, for the reason that if each individual mind were an entirely separate center of perception, not linked to all other minds by a common ground of underlying mentality independent of all individual action, then no two persons would see the same thing at the same time, in fact no two individuals would be conscious of living in the same world. If this were the case there would be no common standard to which to refer our sensations; and, indeed, coming into existence with no consciousness of environment except such as we could form by our own unaided thought, and having by the hypothesis no standard by which to form our thoughts, we could not form the conception of any environment at all, and consequently could have no recognition of our own existence. The confusion of thought involved even in the attempt to state such a condition shows it to be perfectly inconceivable, for the simple reason that it is self-contradictory and self-destructive. On this account it is clear that our own existence and that of the world around us necessarily implies the presence of a Universal Mind acting on certain *fixed lines of its own* which establish the basis for the working of all individual minds. This paramount action of the Universal Mind thus sets an unchangeable standard by which all individual mental action must eventually be measured, and therefore our first concern is to ascertain what this standard is and to make it the basis of our own action.

But if the independent existence of a common standard of reference is necessary for our self-recognition simply as inhabitants of the world we live in, then *a fortiori* a common standard of reference is necessary for our recognition of the unique place we hold in the Creative Order, which is that of introducing the Personal Factor without which the possibilities contained in the great Cosmic Laws would remain undeveloped, and the Self-contemplation of Spirit could never reach those infinite unfoldments of which it is logically capable.

The evolution of the Personal Factor is therefore the point with which we are most concerned. As a matter of fact, whatever theories we may hold to the contrary, we do all realize the same cosmic environment in the same way; that is to say, our minds all act according to certain generic laws which underlie all our individual diversities of thought and feeling. This is so because we are made that way and cannot help it. But with the Personal Factor the case is different. A standard is no less necessary, but we are not so made as to conform to it automatically. The very conception of automatic conformity to a *personal* standard is self-contradictory, for it does away with the very thing that constitutes personality, namely freedom of volition, the use of the powers of Initiative and Selection. For this reason conformity to the Standard of Personality must be a matter of choice, which amounts to the same thing as saying that it rests with each individual to form his own conception of a standard of Personality; but which liberty, however, carries with it the inevitable result that we shall bring into manifestation the *conditions* corresponding to the sort of personality we accept as our normal standard.

I would draw attention to the words "Normal Standard." What we shall eventually attain is, not what we merely wish, but what we regard as normal. The reason is that since we sub-consciously know ourselves to be based upon the inherent Law of the Universal Mind we feel, whether we can reason it out or not, that we cannot force the All-producing Mind to work contrary to its own inherent qualities, and therefore we intuitively recognize that we cannot transcend the sort of personality which is normal according to the Law of Universal Mind. This thought is always at the back of our mind and we cannot get away from it for the simple reason that it is inherent in our mental constitution, because our mind is itself a product of the Creative Process; and to suppose ourselves transcending the possibilities contained in the Originating Mind would involve the absurdity of supposing that we can get the greater out of the less.

Nevertheless there are some who try to do so, and their position is as follows. They say in effect, I want to transcend the standard of humanity as I see it around me. But this is the normal standard according to the Law of the Universe, therefore I have to get above the Law of the Universe. Consequently I cannot draw the necessary power from that Law, and so there is nowhere else to get it except from myself. Thus the aspirant is thrown back upon his own individual will as the ultimate power, with the result that the onus lies on him of concentrating a force sufficient to overcome the Law of the Universe. There is thus continually present to him a suggestion of struggle against a tremendous opposing force, and as a consequence he is continually subjecting himself to a strain which grows more and more intense as he realizes the magnitude of the force against which he is contending. Then as he begins to realize the inequality of the struggle he seeks for extraneous aid, and so he falls back on various expedients, all of which have this in common that they ultimately amount to invoking the assistance of other individualities, not seeing that this involves the same fallacy which has brought him to his present straits, the fallacy, namely, of supposing that any individuality can develop a power greater than that of the source from which itself proceeds. The fallacy is a radical one; and therefore all efforts based upon it are fore-doomed to ultimate failure, whether they take the form of reliance on personal force of will, or magical rites, or austerity practised against the body, or attempts by abnormal concentration to absorb the individual in the universal, or the invocation of spirits, or any other method—the same fallacy is involved in them all, that the less is larger than the greater.

Now the point to be noted is that the idea of transcending the present conditions of humanity does not necessarily imply the idea of

transcending the normal law of humanity. The mistake we have hitherto
made has been in fixing the Standard of Personality too low and in taking
our past experiences as measuring the ultimate possibilities of the race.
Our liberty consists in our ability to form our own conception of the
Normal Standard of Personality, only subject to the conditions arising out
of the inherent Law of the underlying Universal Mind; and so the whole
thing resolves itself into the question, What are those fundamental
conditions? The Law is that we cannot transcend the Normal; therefore
comes the question, What is the Normal?

I have endeavored to answer this question in the chapter on the Divine
Ideal, but since this is the crucial point of the whole subject we may
devote a little further attention to it. The Normal Standard of Personality
must necessarily be the reproduction in Individuality of what the
Universal Mind is in itself, because, by the nature of the Creative Process,
this standard results from Spirit's Self-contemplation at the stage where
its recognition is turned toward its own power of Initiative and Selection.
At this stage Spirit's Self-recognition has passed beyond that of
Self-expression through a mere Law of Averages into the recognition of
what I have ventured to call its Artistic Ability; and as we have seen that
Self-recognition at any stage can only be attained by the realization of a
relation stimulating that particular sort of consciousness, it follows that
for the purpose of this further advance expression through individuals of
a corresponding type is a necessity. Then by the Law of Reciprocity such
beings must possess powers similar to those contemplated in itself by the
Originating Spirit, in other words they must be in their own sphere the
image and likeness of the Spirit as it sees itself.

Now we have seen that the Creating Spirit necessarily possesses the
powers of Initiative and Selection. These we may call its *active*
properties—the summing up of what it *does* . But what any power does
depends on what it *is* , for the simple reason that it cannot give out what
it does not contain; therefore at the back of the initiative and selective
power of the Spirit we must find what the Spirit *is* , namely, what are its
substantive properties. To begin with it must be Life. Then because it is
Life it must be Love, because as the undifferentiated Principle of Life it
cannot do otherwise than tend to the fuller development of life in each
individual, and the pure motive of giving greater enjoyment of life is Love.
Then because it is Life guided by Love it must also be Light, that is to say,
the primary all-inclusive perception of boundless manifestations yet to be.
Then from this proceeds Power, because there is no opposing force at the
level of Pure Spirit; and therefore Life urged forward by Love or the desire
for recognition, and by Light or the pure perception of the Law of Infinite
Possibility, must necessarily produce Power, for the simple reason that
under these conditions it could not stop short of action, for that would be
the denial of the Life, Love, and Light which it is. Then because the Spirit
is Life, Love, Light, and Power, it is also Peace, again for a very simple
reason, that being the Spirit of the Whole it cannot set one part in
antagonism against another, for that would be to destroy the wholeness.
Next the Spirit must be Beauty, because on the same principle of

Wholeness it must duly proportion every part to every other part, and the due proportioning of all parts is beauty. And lastly the Spirit must be Joy, because, working on these lines, it cannot do otherwise than find pleasure in the Self-expression which its works afford it, and in the contemplation of the limitlessness of the Creative Process by which each realized stage of evolution, however excellent, is still the stepping-stone to something yet more excellent, and so on in everlasting progression.

For these reasons we may sum up the Substantive Being of the All-originating Spirit as Life, Love, Light, Power, Peace, Beauty, and Joy; and its Active Power as that of Initiative and Selection. These, therefore, constitute the basic laws of the underlying universal mentality which sets the Standard of Normal Personality—a standard which, when seen in this light, transcends the utmost scope of our thought, for it is nothing else than the Spirit of the Infinite Affirmative conceived in Human Personality. This standard is therefore that of the Universal Spirit itself reproduced in Human Individuality by the same Law of Reciprocity which we have found to be the fundamental law of the Creative Process—only now we are tracing the action of this Law in the Fifth Kingdom instead of in the Fourth.

This Standard, then, we may call the Universal Principle of Humanity, and having now traced the successive steps by which it is reached from the first cosmic movement of the Spirit in the formation of the primary nebula, we need not go over the old ground again, and may henceforward take this Divine Principle of Humanity as our Normal Standard and make it the starting point for our further evolution. But how are we to do this? Simply by using the one method of Creative Process, that is, the Self-contemplation of Spirit. We now know ourselves to be Reciprocals of the Divine Spirit, centers in which It finds a fresh standpoint for Self-contemplation; and so the way to rise to the heights of this Great Pattern is by contemplating it as the Normal Standard of our own Personality.

And be it noted that the Pattern thus set before us is Universal. It is the embodiment of all the great principles of the Affirmative, and so in no way interferes with our own particular individuality—*that* is something built up upon this foundation, something additional affording the differentiating medium through which this unifying Principle finds variety of expression, therefore we need be under no apprehension lest by resting upon this Pattern we should become less ourselves. On the contrary the recognition of it sets us at liberty to become more fully ourselves because we know that we are basing our development, not upon the strength of our own unaided will, nor yet upon any sort of extraneous help, but upon the Universal Law itself, manifesting through us in the proper sequence of the Creative Order; so that we are still dealing with Universal principles, only the principle by which we are now working is the Universal Principle of Personality.

I wish the student to get this idea very clearly because this is really the crux of the passage from the Fourth Kingdom into the Fifth. The great problem of the future of evolution is the introduction of the Personal

Factor. The reason why this is so is very simple when we see it. To take a thought from my own "Doré Lectures" we may put it in this way. In former days no one thought of building ships of iron because iron does not float; yet now ships are seldom built of anything else, though the relative specific gravities of iron and water remain unchanged. What has changed is the Personal Factor. It has expanded to a more intelligent perception of the law of flotation, and we now see that wood floats and iron sinks, both of them by the same principle working under opposite conditions, the law, namely, that anything will float which bulk for bulk is lighter than the volume of water displaced by it, so that by including in our calculations the displacement of the vessel as well as the specific gravity of the material, we now make iron float by the very same law by which it sinks. This example shows that the function of the Personal Factor is to analyze the manifestations of Law which are spontaneously afforded by Nature and to discover the Universal Affirmative Principle which lies hidden within them, and then by the exercise of our powers of Initiative and Selection to provide such specialized conditions as will enable the Universal Principle to work in perfectly new ways transcending anything in our past experience. This is how all progress has been achieved up to the present; and is the way in which all progress must be achieved in the future, only for the purpose of evolution, or growth from within, we must transfer the method to the spiritual plane.

The function, then, of the Personal Factor in the Creative Order is to provide specialized conditions by the use of the powers of Selection and Initiative, a truth indicated by the maxim "Nature unaided fails"; but the difficulty is that if enhanced powers were attained by the whole population of the world without any common basis for their use, their promiscuous exercise could only result in chaotic confusion and the destruction of the entire race. To introduce the creative power of the Individual and at the same time avoid converting it into a devastating flood is the great problem of the transition from the Fourth Kingdom into the Fifth. For this purpose it becomes necessary to have a Standard of the Personal Factor independent of any individual conceptions, just as we found that in order for us to attain self-consciousness at all it was a necessity that there should be a Universal Mind as the *generic* basis of all individual mentality; only in regard to the generic build of mind the conformity is necessarily automatic, while in regard to the specializing process the fact that the essence of that process is Selection and Initiative renders it impossible for the conformity to the Standard of Personality to be automatic—the very nature of the thing makes it a matter of individual choice.

Now a Standard of Personality independent of individual conceptions must be the *essence* of Personality as distinguished from individual idiosyncrasies, and can therefore be nothing else than the Creative Life, Love, Beauty, etc., viewed as a Divine Individuality, by identifying ourselves with which we eliminate all possibility of conflict with other personalities based on the same fundamental recognition; and the very universality of this Standard allows free play to all our particular idiosyncrasies while at the same time preventing them from antagonizing the fundamental principles to which we have found that the Self-contemplation of the Originating Spirit must necessarily give rise. In this way we attain a Standard of Measurement for our own powers. If we recognize no such Standard our development of spiritual powers, our discovery of the immense possibilities hidden in the inner laws of Nature and of our own being, can only become a scourge to ourselves and others, and it is for this reason that these secrets are so jealously guarded by those who know them, and that over the entrance to the temple are written the words "Eskato Bebeloi"—"Hence ye Profane."

But if we recognize and accept this Standard of Measurement then we need never fear our discovery of hidden powers either in ourselves or in Nature, for on this basis it becomes impossible for us to misuse them. Therefore it is that all systematic teaching on these subjects begins with instruction regarding the Creative Order of the Cosmos, and then proceeds to exhibit the same Order as reproduced on the plane of Personality and so affording a fresh starting point for the Creative Process by the introduction of Individual Initiative and Selection. This is the doctrine of the Macrocosm and the Microcosm; and the transition from the generic working of the Creative Spirit in the Cosmos to its specific working in the Individual is what is meant by the doctrine of the Octave.

THE STANDARD OF PERSONALITY

We have now got some general idea as to the place of the personal factor in the Creative Order, and so the next question is, How does this affect ourselves? The answer is that if we have grasped the fundamental fact that the moving power in the Creative Process is the self-contemplation of Spirit, and if we also see that, because we are miniature reproductions of the Original Spirit, our contemplation of It becomes Its contemplation of Itself from the standpoint of our own individuality—if we have grasped these fundamental conceptions, then it follows that our process for developing power is to contemplate the Originating Spirit as the source of the power we want to develop. And here we must guard against a mistake which people often make when looking to the Spirit as the source of power. We are apt to regard it as sometimes giving and sometimes withholding power, and consequently are never sure which way it will act. But by so doing we make Spirit contemplate itself as having no definite action at all, as a plus and minus which mutually cancel each other, and therefore by the Law of the Creative Process no result is to be expected. The mistake consists in regarding the power as something separate from the Spirit; whereas by the analysis of the Creative Process which we have now made we see that the Spirit itself *is* the power, because the power comes into existence only through Spirit's self-contemplation. Then the logical inference from this is that by contemplating the Spirit *as* the power, and *vice versa* by contemplating the power *as* the Spirit, a similar power is being generated in ourselves.

Again an important conclusion follows from this, which is that to generate any *particular sort* of power we should contemplate it in the abstract rather than as applied to the particular set of circumstances we have in hand. The circumstances indicate the sort of power we want but they do not help us to generate it; rather they impress us with a sense of something contrary to the power, something which has to be overcome by it, and therefore we should endeavor to dwell on the power *in itself*, and so come into touch with it in its limitless infinitude.

It is here that we begin to find the benefit of a Divine Standard of Human Individuality. That also is an Infinite Principle, and by identifying ourselves with it we bring to bear upon the abstract conception of infinite Impersonal Power a corresponding conception of Infinite Personality, so that we thus import the Personal Factor which is able *to use* the Power without imposing any strain upon ourselves. We know that by the very nature of the Creative Process we are one with the Originating Spirit and therefore one with all the principles of its Being, and consequently one with its Infinite Personality, and therefore our contemplation of it as the Power which we want gives us the power to use that Power.

This is the Self-contemplation of Spirit employed from the individual standpoint for the generating of power. Then comes the application of the power thus generated. But there is only one Creative Process, that of the Self-contemplation of Spirit, and therefore the way to use this process for the application of the power is to contemplate ourselves as surrounded by the conditions which we want to produce. This does not mean that we are to lay down a hard and fast pattern of the conditions and strenuously endeavor to compel the Power to conform its working to every detail of our mental picture—to do so would be to hinder its working and to exhaust ourselves. What we are to dwell upon is the idea of an Infinite Power producing the happiness we desire, and because this Power is also the Forming Power of the universe trusting it to give that form to the conditions which will most perfectly react upon us to produce the particular state of consciousness desired.

Thus neither on the side of in-drawing nor of out-giving is there any constraining of the Power, while in both cases there is an initiative and selective action on the part of the individual—for the generating of power he takes the initiative of invoking it by contemplation, and he makes selection of the sort of power to invoke; while on the giving-out side he makes selection of the purpose for which the Power is to be employed, and takes the initiative by his thought of directing the Power to that purpose. He thus fulfils the fundamental requirements of the Creative Process by exercising Spirit's inherent faculties of initiative and selection by means of its inherent method, namely by Self-contemplation. The whole action is identical in kind with that which produces the cosmos, and it is now repeated in miniature for the particular world of the individual; only we must remember that this miniature reproduction of the Creative Process is based upon the great fundamental principles inherent in the Universal Mind, and cannot be dissociated from them without involving a conception of the individual which will ultimately be found self-destructive because it cuts away the foundation on which his individuality rests.

It will therefore be seen that any individuality based upon the fundamental Standard of Personality thus involved in the Universal Mind has reached the basic principle of union with the Originating Spirit itself, and we are therefore correct in saying that union is attained through, or by means of, this Standard Personality. This is a great truth which in all ages has been set forth under a variety of symbolic statements; often misunderstood, and still continuing to be so, though owing to the inherent vitality of the idea itself even a partial apprehension of it produces a corresponding measure of good results. This falling short has been occasioned by the failure to recognize an Eternal Principle at the back of the particular statements—in a word the failure to see what they were talking about. All *principles* are eternal in themselves, and this is what distinguishes them from their particular manifestations as laws determined by temporary and local conditions.

If then, we would reach the root of the matter we must penetrate through all verbal statements to an Eternal Principle which is as active now as ever in the past, and which is as available to ourselves as to any who have gone before us. Therefore it is that when we discern an Eternal and Universal Principle of Human Personality as necessarily involved in the Essential Being of the Originating Universal Spirit—*Filius in gremio Patris* —we have discovered the true Normal Standard of Personality. Then because this standard is nothing else than the principle of Personality expanded to infinitude, there is no limit to the expansion which we ourselves may attain by the operation in us of this principle; and so we are never placed in a position of antagonism to the true law of our being, but on the contrary the larger and more fundamental our conception of personal development the greater will be the fulfilment which we give to the Law. The Normal Standard of Personality is found to be itself the Law of the Creative Process working at the personal level; and it cannot be subject to limitation for the simple reason that the process being that of the Self-contemplation of Spirit, no limits can possibly be assigned to this contemplation.

We need, therefore, never be afraid of forming too high an idea of human possibilities provided always that we take this standard as the foundation on which to build up the edifice of our personality. And we see that this standard is no arbitrary one but simply the Expression in Personality of the *One* all-embracing Spirit of the Affirmative; and therefore the only limitation implied by conformity to it is that of being prevented from running on lines the opposite of those of the Creative Process, that is to say, from calling into action causes of disintegration and destruction. In the truly Constructive Order, therefore, the Divine Standard of Personality is as really the basis of the development of specific personality as the Universal Mind is the necessary basis of generic mentality; and just as without this generic ultimate of Mind we should none of us see the same world at the same time, and in fact have no consciousness of existence, so apart from this Divine Standard of Personality it is equally impossible for us to specialize the generic law of our being so as to develop all the glorious possibilities that are latent in it.

Only we must never forget the difference between these two statements of the Universal Law—the one is cosmic and generic, common to the whole race, whether they know it or not, a Standard to which we all conform automatically by the mere fact of being human beings; while the other is a personal and individual Standard, automatic conformity to which is impossible because that would imply the loss of those powers of Initiative and Selection which are the very essence of Personality; so that this Standard necessarily implies a personal selection of it in preference to other conceptions of an antagonistic nature.

RACE THOUGHT AND NEW THOUGHT

The steady following up of the successive stages of the Creative Process has led us to the recognition of an Individuality in the All-creating Spirit itself, but an Individuality which is by its very nature Universal, and so cannot be departed from without violating the essential principles on which the further expansion of our own individuality depends. At the same time it is strictly *individual* , for it is the Spirit of Individuality, and is thus to be distinguished from that merely *generic* race-personality which makes us human beings at all. Race-personality is of course the necessary *basis* for the development of this Individuality; but if we do not see that it is only the preliminary to further evolution, any other conception of our personality as members of the race will prevent our advance toward our proper position in the Creative Order, which is that of introducing the Personal Factor by the exercise of our individual power of initiative and selection.

It is on this account that Race-thought, simply as such, is opposed to the attempt of the individual to pass into a higher order of life. It limits him by strong currents of negative suggestion based on the fallacy that the perpetuation of the race requires the death of the individual;[5] and it is only when the individual sees that this is not true, and that his race-nature constitutes the ground out of which his new Individuality is to be formed, that he becomes able to oppose the negative power of race-thought. He does this by destroying it with its own weapon, that is, by finding in the race-nature itself the very material to be used by the Spirit for building-up the New Man. This is a discovery on the spiritual plane equivalent to the discovery on the physical plane that we can make iron float by the same law by which it sinks. It is the discovery that what we call the mortal part of us is capable of being brought under a higher application of the Universal Law of Life, which will transmute it into an immortal principle. When we see what we call the mortal part of us in this light we can employ the very principle on which the negative race-thought is founded as a weapon for the destruction of that thought in our own minds.

The basis of the negative race-thought is the idea that physical death is an essential part of the Normal Standard of Personality, and that the body is composed of so much neutral material with which death can do what it likes. But it is precisely this neutrality of matter that makes it just as amenable to the Law of Life as to the Law of Death—it is simply neutral and not an originating power on either side; so then when we realize that our Normal Standard of Personality is not subject to death, but is the Eternal Essence and Being of Life itself, then we see that this neutrality of matter—its inability to make selection or take initiative on its own account—is just what makes it the plastic medium for the expression of Spirit in ourselves.

In this way the generic or race-mind in the individual becomes the instrument through which the specializing power of the Spirit works toward the building up of a personality based upon the truly Normal Standard of Individuality which we have found to be inherent in the All-originating Spirit itself: and since the whole question is that of the introduction of the factor of personal individuality into the creative order of causation, this cannot be done by depriving the individual of what makes him a person instead of a thing, namely, the power of conscious initiative and selection.

For this reason the transition from the Fourth Kingdom into the Fifth cannot be forced upon the race either by a Divine fiat or by the generic action of cosmic law, for it is a *specialising* of the cosmic law which can only be effected by *personal* initiative and selection, just as iron can only be made to float under certain specialized conditions; and consequently the passage from the Fourth into the Fifth Kingdom is a strictly individual process which can only be brought about by a personal perception of what the normal standard of the New Individuality really is. This can only be done by the active laying aside of the old race-standard and the conscious adoption of the new one. The student will do well to consider this carefully, for it explains why the race cannot receive the further evolution simply as a race; and also it shows that our further evolution is not into a state of less activity but of greater, not into being less alive but more alive, not into being less ourselves but more ourselves; thus being just the opposite of those systems which present the goal of existence as re-absorption into the undifferentiated Divine essence. On the contrary our further evolution is into greater degrees of conscious activity than we have ever yet known, because it implies our development of greater powers as the consequence of our clearer perception of our true relation to the All-originating Spirit. It is the recognition that we may, and should, measure ourselves by this New Standard instead of by the old race-standard that constitutes the real New Thought. The New Thought which gives New Life to the individual will never be realized so long as we think that it is merely the name of a particular sect, or that it is to be found in the mechanical observance of a set of rules laid down for us by some particular teacher. It is a New Fact in the experience of the individual, the *reason* for which is indeed made clear to him through intellectual perception of the real nature of the Creative Process, but which can become an actual experience only by habitual personal intercourse with that Divine Spirit which is the Life, Love and Beauty that are at the back of the Creative Process and find expression through it.

From this intercourse new thoughts will continually flow in, all of them bearing that vivifying element which is inherent in their source, and the individual will then proceed to work out these new ideas with the knowledge that they have their origin in the selection and initiative power of the All-creating Spirit itself, and in this way by combined meditation and action he will find himself advancing into increasing light, liberty and usefulness. The advance may be almost imperceptible from one day to another, but it will be perceptible at longer intervals, and the one who is thus moving forward with the Spirit of God will on looking back at any time always find that he is getting more livingness out of life than he was a year previously. And this without strenuous effort, for he is not having to manufacture the power from his own resources but only to *receive* it—and as for *using* it, that is only the exercise of the power itself. So following on these lines you will find that Rest and Power are identical; and so you get the real New Thought which grows in Newness every day.

THE DÉNOUEMENT OF THE CREATIVE PROCESS

Then comes the question, What should logically be the dénouement of the progression we have been considering? Let us briefly recapitulate the steps of the series. Universal Spirit by Self-contemplation evolves Universal Substance. From this it produces cosmic creation as the expression of itself as functioning in Space and Time. Then from this initial movement it proceeds to more highly specialized modes of Self-contemplation in a continually ascending scale, for the simple reason that self-contemplation admits of no limits and therefore each stage of self-recognition cannot be other than the starting-point for a still more advanced mode of self-contemplation, and so on *ad infinitum* . Thus there is a continuous progress toward more and more highly specialized forms of life, implying greater liberty and wider scope for enjoyment as the capacity of the individual life corresponds to a higher degree of the contemplation of Spirit; and in this way evolution proceeds till it reaches a level where it becomes impossible to go any further except by the exercise of conscious selection and initiative on the part of the individual, while at the same time conforming to the universal principles of which evolution is the expression.

Now ask yourself in what way individual selection and initiative would be likely to act as expressing the Originating Spirit itself? Given the knowledge on the part of the individual that he is able by his power of initiative and selection to draw directly upon the All-originating Spirit of Life, what motive could he have for not doing so? Therefore, granted such a perfect recognition, we should find the individual holding precisely the same place in regard to his own individual world that the All-originating Spirit does to the cosmos; subject only to the same Law of Love, Beauty, &c., which we found to be necessarily inherent in the Creative Spirit—a similarity which would entirely prevent the individual from exercising his otherwise limitless powers in any sort of antagonism to the Spirit of the Great Whole.

At the same time the individual would be quite aware that he was not the Universal Spirit *in propria persona* , but that he was affording expression to it through his individuality. Now Expression is impossible except through Form, and therefore form of some sort is a necessity of individuality. It is just here, then, that we find the importance of that principle of Harmony with Environment of which I spoke earlier, the principle in accordance with which a person who had obtained complete control of matter, if he wished to transport himself to some other planet, would appear there in perfect conformity with all the laws of matter that obtained in that world; though, of course, not subject to any limitation of the Life Principle in himself. He would exhibit the laws of matter as rendered perfect by the Law of Originating Life. But if any one now living on this earth were thus perfectly to realize the Law of Life he would be in precisely the same position *here* as our imaginary visitor to another planet—in other words the dénouement of the Law of Life is not the putting off of the body, but its inclusion as part of the conscious life of the Spirit.

This does not imply any difference in the molecular structure of the body from that of other men, for by the principle of Harmony of which I have just spoken, it would be formed in strict accordance with the laws of matter on the particular planet; though it would not be subject to the limitations resulting from the average man's non-recognition of the power of the Spirit. The man who had thus fully entered into the Fifth Kingdom would recognize that, in its relation to the denser modes of matter his body was of a similar dense mode. That would be its relation to external environment as seen by others. But since the man now knew *himself* as not belonging to these denser modes of manifestation, but as an individualization of Primary Spirit, he would see that relatively to himself all matter was Primary Substance, and that from this point of view any condensations of that substance into atoms, molecules, tissues, and the like counted for nothing—for him the body would be simply Primary Substance entirely responsive to his will. Yet his reverence for the Law of Harmony would prevent any disposition to play psychic pranks with it, and he would use his power over the body only to meet actual requirements.

In this way, then, we are led to the conclusion that eternal life in an immortal physical body is the logical dénouement of our evolution; and if we reflect that, by the conditions of the case, the owners of such bodies could at will either transport themselves to other worlds or put off the physical body altogether and remain in the purely subjective life while still retaining the power to reclothe themselves in flesh whenever they chose, we shall see that this dénouement of evolution answers all possible questions as to the increase of the race, the final destruction of the planet, and the like.

This, then, is the ultimate which we should keep in view; but the fact remains that, though there may be hidden ones who have thus attained, the bulk of mankind have not, and that the common lot of humanity is to go through the change which we call death. In broad philosophical terms death may be described as the withdrawal of the life into the subjective consciousness to the total exclusion of the objective consciousness. Then by the general law of the relation between subjective and objective mind, the subjective mind severed from its corresponding objective mentality has no means of acquiring fresh impressions *on its own account* , and therefore can only ring the changes on those impressions which it has brought with it from its past life. But these may be of very various sorts, ranging from the lowest to the highest, from those most opposed to that ultimate destiny of man which we have just been considering, to those which recognize his possibilities in a very large measure, needing little more to bring about the full fruition of perfected life. But however various may be their experiences, all who have passed through death must have this in common that they have lost their physical instrument of objective perception and so have their mode of consciousness determined entirely by the dominant mode of suggestion which they have brought over with them from the objective side of life.[6] Of course if the objective mentality were also brought over this would give the individual the same power of initiative and selection that he possesses while in the body, and, as we shall see later on, there are exceptional persons with whom this is the case; but for the great majority the physical brain is a necessity for the working of the objective mentality, and so when they are deprived of this instrument their life becomes purely subjective and is a sort of dream-life, only with a vast difference between two classes of dreamers—those who dream as they must and those who dream as they will. The former are those who have enslaved themselves in various ways to their lower mentality—some by bringing with them the memory of crimes unpardoned, some by bringing with them the idea of a merely animal life, others less degraded, but still in bondage to limited thought, bringing with them only the suggestion of a frivolous worldly life—in this way, by the natural operation of the Law of Suggestion, these different classes, either through remorse, or unsatisfied desires, or sheer incapacity to grasp higher principles, all remain earth-bound, suffering in exact correspondence with the nature of the suggestion they have brought along with them. The unchangeable Law is that the suggestion becomes the life; and this is equally true of suggestions of a happier sort. Those who have brought over with them the great truth that conditions are the creations of thought, and who have accustomed themselves while in objective life to dwell on good and beautiful ideas, are still able, by reason of being imbued with this suggestion, to mold the conditions of their consciousness in the subjective world in accordance with the sort of ideas which have become a second nature to them. Within the limits of these ideas the dominant suggestion to these entities is that of a Law which confers Liberty, so by using this Law of the constructive power of thought they can determine the conditions of their own consciousness; and thus instead of being compelled to suffer the nightmare dreams of the other class, they can mold their dream according to their will. We cannot conceive of such a life as theirs in the unseen as otherwise than happy, nevertheless its range is limited by the range of the conceptions they have brought with them. These may be exceedingly beautiful and thoroughly true and logical *as far as they go* ; but they do not go the whole way, otherwise these spirits would not be in the category which we are considering but would belong to that still higher class who fully realize the ultimate possibilities which the Law of the Expression of Spirit provides.

The otherwise happy subjective life of these more enlightened souls has this radical defect that they have failed to bring over with them that power of original selection and initiative without which further progress is impossible. I wish the student to grasp this point very clearly, for it is of the utmost importance. Of course the basis of our further evolution is conformity to the harmonious nature of the Originating Spirit; but upon this foundation we each have to build up the superstructure of our own individuality, and every step of advance depends on our personal development of power to take that step. This is what is meant by taking an initiative. It is making a New Departure, not merely recombining the old things into fresh groupings still subject to the old laws, but introducing an entirely new element which will bring its own New Law along with it.

Now if this is the true meaning of "initiative" then that is just the power which these otherwise happy souls do not possess. For by the very conditions of the case they are living only in their subjective consciousness, and consequently are living by the law of subjective mind; and one of the chief characteristics of subjective mind is its incapacity to reason inductively, and therefore its inability to make the selection and take the initiative necessary to inaugurate a New Departure. The well established facts of mental law show conclusively that subjective mind argues only deductively. It argues quite correctly from any given premises, but it cannot take the initiative in selecting the premises—that is the province of inductive reasoning which is essentially the function of the objective mind. But by the law of Auto-suggestion this discarnate individual has brought over his premises with him, which premises are the sum-total of his inductions made during objective life, the conception of things which he held at the time he passed over, for this constituted his idea of Truth. Now he cannot add to these inductions, for he has parted with his instrument for inductive reasoning, and therefore his deductive reasoning in the purely subjective state which he has now entered is necessarily limited to the consequences which may be deducted from the premises which he has brought along with him.

In the case of the highly-developed individualities we are now considering the premises thus brought over are of a very far-reaching and beautiful character, and consequently the range of their subjective life is correspondingly wide and beautiful; but, nevertheless, it is subject to the radical defect that it is debarred from further progress for the simple reason that the individual has not brought over with him the mental faculty which can impress his subjective entity with the requisite forward movement for making a new departure into a New Order. And moreover, the higher the subjective development with which the individual passed over the more likely he will be to realize this defect. If during earth-life he had gained sufficient knowledge of these things he will carry with him the knowledge that his discarnate existence is purely subjective; and therefore he will realize that, however he may be able to order the pictures of his dream, yet it is still but a dream, and in common with all other dreams lacks the basis of solidity from which to take *really creative action* .

He knows also that the condition of other discarnate individualities is similar to his own, and that consequently each one must necessarily live in a world apart—a world of his own creation, because none of them possess the objective mentality by which to direct their subjective currents so as to make them penetrate into the sphere of another subjective entity, which is the *modus operandi* of telepathy. Thus he is conscious of his own inability to hold intercourse with other personalities; for though he may for his own pleasure create the semblance of them in his dream-life, yet he knows that these are creations of his own mind, and that while he appears to be conversing with a friend amid the most lovely surroundings the friend himself may be having experiences of a very different description. I am, of course, speaking now of persons who have passed over in a very high state of development and with a very considerable, though still imperfect, knowledge of the Law of their own being. Probably the majority take their dream-life for an external reality; and, in any case, all who have passed over without carrying their objective mentality along with them must be shut up in their individual subjective spheres and cease to function as centers of creative power so long as they do not emerge from that state.

But the highly advanced individuals of whom I am now speaking have passed over with a true knowledge of the Law of the relation between subjective and objective mind and have therefore brought with them a *subjective* knowledge of this truth; and therefore, however otherwise in a certain sense happy, they must still be conscious of a fundamental limitation which prevents their further advance. And this consciousness can produce only one result, an ever-growing longing for the removal of this limitation—and this represents the intense desire of the Spirit, as individualized in these souls, to attain to the conditions under which it can freely exercise its creative power. Sub-consciously this is the desire of *all* souls, for it is that continual pressing forward of the Spirit for manifestation out of which the whole Creative Process arises; and so it is that the great cry perpetually ascends to God from all as yet undelivered souls, whether in or out of the body, for the deliverance which they knowingly or unknowingly desire.

All this comes out of the well-ascertained facts of the law of relation between subjective and objective mind. Then comes the question, Is there no way of getting out of this law? The answer is that we can never get away from universal principles—*but we can specialise them*. We may take it as an axiom that any law which appears to limit us contains in itself the principle by which that limitation can be overcome, just as in the case of the flotation of iron. In this axiom, then, we shall find the clue which will bring us out of the labyrinth. The same law which places various degrees of limitation upon the souls that have passed into the invisible can be so applied as to set them free. We have seen that everything turns on the obligation of our subjective part to act within the limits of the suggestion which has been most deeply impressed upon it. Then why not impress upon it the suggestion that in passing over to the other side it has brought its objective mentality along with it?

If such a suggestion were effectively impressed upon our subjective mind, then by the fundamental law of our nature our subjective mind would act in strict accordance with this suggestion, with the result that the objective mind would no longer be separated from it, and that we should carry with us into the unseen our *whole* mentality, both subjective and objective, and so be able to exercise our inductive powers of selection and initiative as well there as here.

Why not? The answer is that we cannot accept any suggestion unless we believe it to be true, and to believe it to be true we must feel that we have a solid foundation for our belief. If, then, we can find a sufficient foundation for adequately impressing this suggestion upon ourselves, then the principles of mental law assure us that we shall carry our objective faculty of initiative and selection into the unseen. Therefore our quest is to find this Foundation. Then, since we cannot accept as true what we believe to be contrary to the ultimate law of the universe, if we are to find such a foundation at all it must be within that Law; and it is for this reason that I have laid so much stress upon the Normal Standard of Human Individuality. When we are convinced that this ideal completeness is quite normal, and is a spiritual fact, not dependent upon the body, but able to control the body, then we have got the solid basis on which to carry our objective personality along with us into the unseen, and the well-established laws of our mental constitution justify the belief that we can do so.

From these considerations it is obvious that those who thus pass over in possession of their complete mentality must be in a very different position from those who pass into a condition of merely subjective life, for they have brought their powers of selection and initiative with them, and can therefore employ their experiences in the unseen as a starting-point for still further development. So, then, the question arises, What lines will this further development be likely to follow?

We are now considering the case of persons who have reached a very high degree of development; who have succeeded in so completely uniting the subjective and objective portions of their spiritual being into a perfect whole that they can never again be severed; and who are therefore able to function with their whole consciousness on the spiritual plane. Such persons will doubtless be well aware that they have attained this degree of development by the Law of the Creative Process working in terms of their own individuality, and so they would naturally always refer to the original Cosmic Creation as the demonstration of the principle which they have to specialize for their own further evolution. Then they would find that the principle involved is that of the manifestation of Spirit in Form; and they would further see that this manifestation is not an illusion but a reality, for the simple reason that both mind and matter are equally projections from the Great Originating Spirit. Both alike are thoughts of the Divine Mind, and it is impossible to conceive any greater reality than the Divine Thought, or to get at any more substantial source of reality than that. Even if we were to picture the Divine Mind as laughing at its productions as being mere illusions *relatively to itself* (which I certainly do not), still the relation between the individual mind and material existence would be a reality for the individual, on the simple mathematical ground that like signs multiplied together invariably produce a positive result, even though the signs themselves be negative;

so that, for us, at every stage of our existence substance must always be as much a reality as mind. Therefore the manifestation of Spirit in Form is the eternal principle of the Creative Process whether in the evolution of a world-system or in that of an individual.

But when we realize that by the nature of the Creative Process substance must be an eternal verity we must not suppose that this is true also of *particular forms* or of *particular modes* of matter. Substance is a necessity for the expression of Spirit, but it does not follow that Spirit is tied down to any particular mode of expression. If you fold a piece of paper into the form of a dart it will fly through the air by the law of the form which you have given it. Again, if you take the same bit of paper and fold it into the shape of a boat it will float on water by the law of the new form that you have given it. The thing formed will act in accordance with the form given it, and the same paper can be folded into different forms; but if there were no paper you could put it into any shape at all. The dart and the boat are both real so long as you retain the paper in either of those shapes; but this does not alter the fact that you can change the shapes, though your power to do so depends on the existence of the paper. This is a rough analogy of the relation between ultimate substance and particular forms, and shows us that neither substance nor shape is an illusion; both are essential to the manifestation of Spirit, only by the nature of the Creative Process the Spirit has power to determine what shape substance shall take at any particular time.

Accordingly we find the great Law that, as Spirit is the Alpha of the Creative Process, so solid material Form is its Omega; in other words the Creative Series is incomplete until solid material form is reached. Anything short of this is a condition of incompleteness, and therefore the enlightened souls who have passed over in possession of both sides of their mentality will realize that their condition, however beatific, is still one of incompleteness; and that what is wanted for completion is expression through a material body. This, then, is the direction in which such souls would use their powers of initiative and selection as being the true line of evolution—in a word they would realize that the principle of Creative Progression, when it reaches the level of fully developed mental man, necessarily implies the Resurrection of the Body, and that anything short of this would be retrogression and not progress.

At the same time persons who had passed over with this knowledge would never suppose that Resurrection meant merely the resuscitation of the old body under the old conditions; for they would see that the same inherent law which makes expression in concrete substance the ultimate of the creative series also makes this ultimate form depend on the originating movement of the spirit which produces it, and therefore that, although *some* concrete form is essential for complete manifestation, and is a substantial reality so long as it is maintained, yet the maintaining of the particular form is entirely dependent on the action of the spirit of which the form is the external clothing. This resurrection body would therefore be no mere illusory spirit-shape, yet it would not be subject to the limitations of matter as we now know it: it would be physical matter still, but entirely subject to the will of the indwelling spirit, which would not regard the denser atomic relations of the body but only its absolute and essential nature as Primary Substance. I want the student to grasp the idea that the same thing may be very different when looked at, so to say, from opposite ends of the stick. What is solid molecular matter when viewed from the outside is plastic primary substance when viewed from the inside. The relations of this new body to any stimulus proceeding from outside would be those of the external laws of Nature; but its relation to the spiritual ego working from within would be that of a plastic substance to be molded at will. The employment of such power would, however, at all times be based upon the reverent worship of the All-creating Spirit; and it would therefore never be exercised otherwise than in accordance with the harmonious progress of the Creative Process. Proceeding on these lines the spirit in the individual would stand in precisely the same relation to his body that the All-originating Spirit does to the cosmos.

This, then, is the sort of body which the instructed would contemplate as that in which he was to attain resurrection. He would regard it, not as an illusion, but as a great reality; while at the same time he would not need to trouble himself about its particular form, for he would know that it would be the perfect expression of his own conception of himself. He would know this because it is in accordance with the fundamental principle that external creation has its root in the Self-contemplation of Spirit.

Those passing over with this knowledge would obviously be in a very different position from those who passed over with only a subjective consciousness. They would bring with them powers of selection and initiative by which they could continue to impress fresh and expanding conceptions upon their subjective mind, and so cause it to carry on its work as the seed-ground of the whole individuality, instead of being shut up in itself as a mere circulus for the repetition of previously received ideas; and so in their recognition of the *principle* of physical resurrection they would have a clear and definite line of auto-suggestion. And because this suggestion is derived from the undeniable facts of the whole cosmic creation, it is one which both subjective and objective mind can accept as an established fact, and so the suggestion becomes effective. This suggestion, then, becomes the self-contemplation of the individual spirit; and because it is in strict conformity with the generic principle of the Original Creative Activity, of which the individual mind is itself a product, this becomes also the Self-contemplation of the Originating Spirit as seeing itself reflected in the individual spirit; so that, by the basic law of the Creative Process, this suggestion is bound sooner or later to work out into its corresponding fact, namely, the production of a material body free from the power of death and from all those limitations which we now associate with our physical organism.

This, then, is the hope of those who pass over in recognition of the great truth. But how about those who have passed over without that recognition? We have seen that their purely subjective condition precludes them from taking any initiative on their own account, for that requires the presence of objective mind. Their subjective mind, however, still retains its essential nature; that is, it is still susceptible to suggestion, and still possesses its inherent creativeness in working out any suggestion that is sufficiently deeply implanted in it. Here, then, opens up a vast field of activity for that other class who have passed over in possession of both sides of their mentality. By means of their powers of initiative and selection they can on the principle of telepathy cause their own subjective mind to penetrate the subjective spheres of those who do not possess those powers, and they can thus endeavor to impress upon them the great truth of the physical ultimate of the Creative Process—the truth that any series which stops short of that ultimate is incomplete, and, if insisted upon as being ultimate, must become self-destructive because in opposition to the inherent working of the Universal Creative Spirit. Then, as the perception of the true nature of the Creative Process dawned upon any subjective entity, it would by reason of accepting this suggestion begin to develop an objective mentality, and so would gradually attain to the same status as those who had passed over in full possession of all their mental powers.

But the more the objective mentality became developed in these discarnate personalities the more the need of a corresponding physical instrument would assert itself, both from their intellectual perception of the original cosmic process, and also from the inherent energy of the Spirit as centered in the ultimate ego of the individual. Not to seek material manifestation would be the contrary of all we have traced out regarding the nature of the Creative Process; and hence the law of tendency resulting from the conscious union of subjective and objective mind in the individual must necessarily be toward the production of a physical form. Only we must recollect, as I have already pointed out, that this concentration of these minds would be upon a principle and not upon a particular bodily shape. The particular form they would be content to leave to the inherent self-expressiveness of the Universal Spirit working through the particular ego, with the result that their expectation would be fixed upon a *general principle* of physical Resurrection which would provide a form suited to be the material instrument of the highest ideal of man as a spiritual and mental being. Then, since the subjective mind is the automatic builder of the body, the result of the individual's acceptance of the Resurrection principle must be that this mental conception will eventually work out as a corresponding fact. Whether on this planet or on some other, matters not, for, as we have already seen, the physical body evolved by a soul that is conscious of its unity with the Universal Spirit is bound to be in conformity with the physical laws of *any* planet, though from the standpoint of the conscious ego not limited by them.

In this way we may conceive that those who have passed over in possession of both sides of their spiritual nature would find a glorious field of usefulness in the unseen in helping to emancipate those who had passed over in possession of their subjective side only. But from our present analysis it will be seen that this can only be effected on the basis of a recognition of the principle of the Resurrection of the Body. Apart from the recognition of this principle the only possible conception which the discarnate individual could form of himself would be that of a purely subjective being; and this carries with it all the limitations of a subjective life unbalanced by an objective one; and so long as the principle of physical resurrection is denied, so long the life must continue to be merely subjective and consequently unprogressive.[7]

But it may be asked why those who have realized this great principle sufficiently to carry their objective mentality into the unseen state are liable to the change which we call death. The answer is that though they have realized *the general principle* they have not yet divested themselves of certain conceptions by which they limit it, and consequently by the law of subjective mind they carry those limitations into the working of the Resurrection principle itself.

They are limited by the race-belief that physical death is under all conditions a necessary law of Nature, or by the theological belief that death is the will of God; so then the question is whether these beliefs are well founded. Of course appeal is made to universal experience, but it does not follow that the universal experience of the past is bound to be the universal experience of the future—the universal experience of the past was that no man had ever flown across the English Channel, yet now it has been done. What we have to do, therefore, is not to bother about past experience, but to examine the inherent nature of the Law of Life and see whether it does not contain possibilities of further development. And the first step in this direction is to see whether what we have hitherto considered limitations of the law are really integral parts of the law itself. The very statement of this question shows the correct answer; for how can a force acting in one direction be an integral part of a force acting in the opposite direction? How can the force which pulls a thing down be an integral part of the force which builds it up? To suppose, therefore, that the limitations of the law are an integral portion of the law itself is a *reductio ad absurdum*.

For these reasons the argument from the past experience of the race counts for nothing; and when we examine the theological argument we shall find that it is only the old argument from past experience in another dress. It is alleged that death is the will of God. How do we know that it is the will of God? Because the facts prove it so, is the ultimate answer of all religious systems with one exception; so here we are back again at the old race-experience as the criterion of truth. Therefore the theological argument is nothing but the materialistic argument disguised. It is in our more or less *conscious* acceptance of the materialistic argument, under any of its many disguises, that the limitation of life is to be found—not in the Law of Life itself; and if we are to bring into manifestation the infinite possibilities latent in that Law it can only be by looking steadily into the *principle* of the Law and resolutely denying everything that opposes it. The Principle of Life must of necessity be Affirmative, and affirmative throughout, without any negative anywhere—if we once realize this we shall be able to unmask the enemy and silence his guns.

Now to do this is precisely the one object of the Bible; and it does it in a thoroughly logical manner, always leading on to the ultimate result by successive links of cause and effect. People will tell you that the Bible is their authority for saying that Death is the will of God; but these are people who read it carelessly; and ultimately the only reason they can give you for their manner of interpreting the Bible is that the facts prove their interpretation to be correct; so that in the last resort you will always find you have got back to the old materialistic argument from past race-experience, which logically proves nothing. These are good well-meaning people with a limited idea which they read into the Bible, and so limit its promises by making physical death an essential preliminary to Resurrection. They grasp, of course, the great central idea that Perfected Man possesses a joyous immortal Life permeating spirit, soul and body; but they relegate it to some dim and distant future, entirely disconnected from the present law of our being, not seeing that if we are to have eternal life it must necessarily be involved in some principle which is eternal, and therefore existing, at any rate latently, at the present moment. Hence, though their fundamental principle is true, they are all the time mentally limiting it, with the result that they themselves create the conditions they impose upon it, and consequently the principle will work (as principles always do) in accordance with the conditions provided for its action.

Unless, therefore, this limiting belief is entirely eradicated, the individual, though realizing the fundamental principle of Life, is bound to pass out of physical existence; but on the other hand, since he does take the recognition of this fundamental principle with him, it is bound to bear fruit sooner or later in a joyous Resurrection, while the intermediate state can only be a peaceful anticipation of that supreme event. This is the answer to the question why those who have realized the great principle sufficiently to carry their objective mentality into the unseen world are still liable to physical death; and in the last analysis it will be found to resolve itself into the remains of race belief based upon past experience. These are they who pass over in sure and certain hope of a glorious Resurrection—sure and certain because founded upon the very Being of God Himself, that inherent Life of the All-creating Divine Spirit which is the perpetual interaction of the Eternal Love and Beauty. They have grasped the Life-giving Truth, only they have postponed its operation, because they have the fixed idea that its present fruition is an absolute impossibility.

But if we ask the reason for this idea it always comes back to the old materialistic argument from the experience of past conditions, while the whole nature of advance is in the opening up of new conditions. And in this advance the Bible is the pioneer book. Its whole purport is to tell us most emphatically that death is *not* the will of God. In the story of Eden God is represented as warning man of the poisonous nature of the forbidden fruit, which is incompatible with the idea of death as an essential feature of man's nature. Then from the point where man has taken the poison all the rest of the Bible is devoted to telling us how to get rid of it. Christ, it tells us, was manifested to bring Life and Immortality to light—to abolish death—to destroy the works of the devil, that is the death-dealing power, for "he that hath the power of death is the devil." It is impossible to reconcile this life-giving conception of the Bible with the idea that death at any stage or in any degree is the desire of God. Let us, therefore, start with the recognition that this negative force, whether in its minor degrees as disease or in its culmination as death, is that which it is the will of God to abolish. This also is logical; for if God be the Universal Spirit of Life finding manifestation in individual lives, how can the desire of this Spirit be to act in opposition to its own manifestation? Therefore Scripture and common-sense alike assure us that the will of God toward us is Life and not death.[8]

We may therefore start on our quest for Life with the happy certainty that God is on our side. But people will meet us with the objection that though God wills Life to us, He does not will it just yet, but only in some dim far-off future. How do we know this? Certainly not from the Bible. In the Bible Jesus speaks of two classes of persons who believe on Him as the Manifestation or Individualisation of the Spirit of Life. He speaks of those who, having passed through death, still believe on Him, and says that these *shall* live—a future event. And at the same time He speaks of those who are living and believe on Him, and says that they shall never die—thus contemplating the entire elimination of the contingency of death (John xi. 25).

Again St. Paul expresses his wish not to be unclothed but to be clothed upon, which he certainly would not have done had he considered the latter alternative a nonsensical fancy. And in another place he expressly states that we shall not all die, but that some shall be transmuted into the Resurrection body without passing through physical death. And if we turn to the Old Testament we find two instances in which this is said to have actually occurred, those of Enoch and Elijah. And we may note in passing that the Bible draws our attention to certain facts about these two personages which are important as striking at the root of the notion that austerities of some sort are necessary for the great attainment. Of Enoch we are expressly told that he was the father of a large family, and of Elijah that he was a man of like nature with ourselves—thus showing us what is wanted is not a shutting of ourselves off from ordinary human life but such a clear realization of the Universal Principle, of which our personal life is the more or less conscious manifestation, that our commonest actions will be hallowed by the Divine Presence; and so the grand dénouement will be only the natural result of our daily habit of walking with God. From the stand-point of the Bible, therefore, the attainment of physical regeneration without passing through death is not an impossibility, nor is it necessarily relegated to some far off future. Whatever any one else may say to the contrary, the Bible contemplates such a dénouement of human evolution as a present possibility.

Then if we argue from the philosophical stand-point we arrive at precisely the same result. Past experience proves nothing, and we must therefore make a fresh start by going back to the Original Creative action of the Spirit of Life itself. Then, if we take this as our starting point, remembering that at the stage of this *original* movement there can be no intervention by a second power, because there is none, why should we mentally impose any restriction upon the action of the Creative Power? Certainly not by its own Law of Tendency, for that must always be toward fuller self-expression; and since this can only take place through the individual, the desire of the Spirit must always be toward the increasing of the individual life. Nor yet from anything in the created substance, for that would either be to suppose the Spirit creating something in limitation of its own Self-expression, or else to suppose that the limiting substance was created by some other power working against the Spirit; and as this would mean a Duality of powers we should not have reached the Originating Power at all, and so we might put Spirit and Substance equally out of court as both being merely modes of secondary causation. But if we see that the Universal Substance must be created by emanation from the Universal Spirit, then we see that no limitation of Spirit by substance is possible. We may therefore feel assured that no limitation proceeds either from the will of the Spirit or from the nature of Substance.

Where, then, does limitation come from? Limiting conditions are created by the same power which creates everything else, namely, the Self-contemplation of Spirit. This is why it is so important to realize that the individual mind forms a center from which the self-contemplating action of Spirit is specialized in terms of the individual's own mode of thinking, and therefore so long as the individual contemplates negative conditions as being *of the essence* of his own personality, he is in effect employing the Creative Power of the Self-contemplation of Spirit invertedly, destructively instead of constructively. The Law of the Self-contemplation of Spirit as the Creative Power is as true in the microcosm as in the macrocosm, and so the individual's contemplation of himself as subject to the law of sin and death keeps him subject to that law, while the opposite self-contemplation, the contemplation of himself as rejoicing in the Life of the Spirit, the Perfect Law of Liberty, must necessarily produce the opposite results.

Why, then, should not regeneration be accomplished here and now? I can see no reason against it, either Scriptural or philosophical, except our own difficulty in getting rid of the race-traditions which are so deeply embedded in our subjective minds. To get rid of these we require a firm basis on which to receive the opposite suggestion. We need to be convinced that our ideal of a regenerated self is in accord with the Normal Standard of Humanity and is within the scope of the laws of the universe. Now to make clear to us the *infinitude* of the truly Normal Standard of Humanity is the whole purpose of the Bible; and the Manifestation of this Standard is set before us in the Central Personality of the Scriptures who is at once the Son of God and the Son of Man—the Great Exception, if you will, to man as we know him now, but the Exception which proves the Rule. In proportion as we begin to realize this we begin to introduce into our own life the action of that Personal Factor on which all further development depends; and when our recognition is complete we shall find that we also are children of God.

CONCLUSION

We are now in a position to see the place occupied by the individual in the Creative Order. We have found that the originating and maintaining force of the whole Creative Process is the Self-contemplation of the Spirit, and that this necessarily produces a Reciprocal corresponding to the idea embodied in the contemplation, and thus manifesting that idea in a correlative Form. We have found that in this way the externalization of the idea progresses from the condensation of the primary nebula to the production of human beings as a race, and that at this point the simple *generic* reproduction of the idea terminates. This means that up to, and including, *genus homo* , the individual, whether plant, animal, or man, is what it is simply by reason of race conditions and not by exercise of deliberate choice. Then we have seen that the next step in advance must necessarily be by the individual becoming aware that he has power to mold the conditions of his own consciousness and environment by the creative power of his thought; thus not only enabling him to take a conscious part in his own further evolution but precluding him from evolving any further except by the right exercise of this power; and we have found that the crux of the passage from the Fourth to the Fifth Kingdom is to get people so to understand the nature of their creative power as not to use it destructively. Now what we require to see is that the Creative Process has always only one way of working, and that is by Reciprocity or Reflection, or, as we might say, by the law of Action and Re-action, the re-action being always equivalent and correspondent to the action which generated it. If this Law of Reciprocity be grasped then we see how the progress of the Creative Process must at length result in producing a being who himself possesses the power of independent spiritual initiative and is thus able to carry on the creative work from the stand-point of his own individuality.

Now the great crux is first to get people to see that they possess this power at all, and then to get them to use it in the right direction. When our eyes begin to open to the truth that we do possess this power the temptation is to ignore the fact that our power of initiative is itself a product of the similar power subsisting in the All-originating Spirit. If this origin of our own creative faculty is left out of sight we shall fail to recognize the Livingness of the Greater Life within which we live. We shall never get nearer to it than what we may call its *generic* level, the stage at which the Creative Power is careful of the type or race but is careless of the individual; and so at this level we shall never pass into the Fifth Kingdom which is the Kingdom of Individuality—we have missed the whole point of the transition to the more advanced mode of being, in which the individual consciously functions as a creative center, because we have no conception of a Universal Power that works at any higher level than the generic, and consequently to reach a specific personal exercise of creative power we should have to conceive of ourselves as transcending the Universal Law. But if we realize that our own power of creative initiative has its origin in the similar faculty of the All-Originating Mind then we see that the way to maintain the Life-giving energy in ourselves is to use our power of spiritual initiative so as to impress upon the Spirit the conception of ourselves as standing related to It in a specific, individual, and personal way that takes us out of the mere category of *genus homo* and gives us a specific spiritual individuality of our own. Thus our mental action produces a corresponding re-action in the mind of the Spirit, which in its turn reproduces itself as a special manifestation of the Life of the Spirit in us; and so long as this circulation between the individual spirit and the Great Spirit is kept up, the individual life will be maintained, and will also strengthen as the circulation continues, for the reason that the Spirit, as the Original Creative Power, is a Multiplying Force, and the current sent into it is returned multiplied, just as in telegraphy the feeble current received from a distance at the end of a long line operates to start a powerful battery in the receiving office, which so multiplies the force as to give out a clear message, which but for the multiplication of the original movement could not have been done. Something like this we may picture the multiplying tendency of the Originating Mind, and consequently the longer the circulation between it and the individual mind goes on the stronger the latter becomes; and this process growing habitual becomes at last automatic, thus producing an endless flow of Life continually expanding in intelligence, love, power and joy.

But we must note carefully that all this can only proceed from the individual's recognition that his own powers are a derivative from the All-originating Spirit, and that they can continue to be used constructively only so long as they are employed in harmony with the inherent Forward Movement of the Spirit. Therefore to insure this eternally flowing stream of Life from the Universal Spirit into the individual there must be *no inversion* in the individual's presentation of himself to the Originating Power: for through the very same Law by which we seek Life—the Life namely, of reciprocal action and re-action—every inversion we bring with us in presenting ourselves to the Spirit is bound to be faithfully reproduced in a corresponding re-action, thus adulterating the stream of Pure Life, and rendering it less life-giving in proportion to the extent to which we invert the action of the Life-principle; so that in extreme cases the stream flowing through and from the individual may be rendered absolutely poisonous and deadly, and the more so the greater his recognition of his own personal power to employ spiritual forces.

The existence of these negative possibilities in the spiritual world should never be overlooked, and therefore the essential condition for receiving the Perfect Fulness of Life is that we should present ourselves before the Eternal Spirit free from every trace of inversion. To do this means to present ourselves in the likeness of the Divine Ideal; and in this self-presentation the initiative, so far as the individual is consciously concerned, must necessarily be taken by himself. He is to project into the Eternal Mind the conception of himself as identical with its Eternal Ideal; and if he can do this, then by the Law of the Creative Process a return current will flow from the Eternal Mind reproducing this image in the individual with a continually growing power. Then the question is, How are we to do this?

The answer is that to take the initiative for inducing this flow of Life individually it is a *sine qua non* that the conditions enabling us to do so should first be presented to us universally. This is in accordance with the general principle that we can never create a force but can only specialize it. Only here the power we are wanting to specialize is the very Power of Specialization itself; and therefore, paradoxical as it may seem, what we require to have shown us is the Universality of Specialization.

Now this is what the Bible puts before us in its central figure. Taking the Bible statements simply and literally they show us this unique Personality as the Principle of Humanity, alike in its spiritual origin and its material manifestation, carried to the logical extreme of specialization; while at the same time, as the embodiment of the original polarity of Spirit and Substance, this Personality, however unique, is absolutely universal; so that the Bible sets Jesus Christ before us as the answer to the philosophic problem of how to specialize the universal, while at the same time preserving its universality.

If, then, we fix our thought upon this unique Personality as the embodiment of *universal* principles, it follows that those principles must exist in ourselves also, and that His actual specialization of them is the earnest of our potential specialization of them. Then if we fix our thought on this potential in ourselves as being identical with its manifestation in Him, we can logically claim our identity with Him, so that what He has done we have done, what He is, we are, and thus recognizing ourselves in Him we present *this* image of ourselves to the Eternal Mind, with the result that we bring with us no inversion, and so import no negative current into our stream of Life.

Thus it is that we reach "the Father" through "the Son," and that He is able to keep us from falling and to present us faultless before the presence of the Divine glory with exceeding joy (Jude 24). The Gospel of "the Word made flesh" is not the meaningless cant of some petty sect nor yet the cunning device of priestcraft, though it has been distorted in both these directions; but it can give a reason for itself, and is founded upon the deepest laws of the threefold constitution of man, embracing the *whole* man, body, soul and spirit. It is not opposed to Science but is the culmination of all science whether physical or mental. It is philosophical and logical throughout if you start the Creative Process where alone it can start, in the Self-contemplation of the Spirit. The more carefully we examine into the claims of the Gospel of Christ the more we shall find all the current objections to it melt away and disclose their own superficialness. We shall find that Christ is indeed the Mediator between God and Man, not by the arbitrary fiat of a capricious Deity, but by a logical law of sequence which solves the problem of making extremes meet, so that the Son of Man is also the Son of God; and when we see the reason why this is so we thereby receive power to become ourselves sons of God, which is the dénouement of the Creative Process in the Individual.

These closing lines are not the place to enter upon so great a subject, but I hope to follow it up in another volume and to show in detail the logic of the Bible teaching, what it saves us from and what it leads us to; to show while giving due weight to the value of other systems how it differs from them and transcends them; to glance, perhaps, for a moment at the indications of the future and to touch upon some of the dangers of the present and the way to escape from them. Nor would I pass over in silence another and important aspect of the Gospel contained in Christ's commission to His followers to heal the sick. This also follows logically from the Law of the Creative Process if we trace carefully the sequence of connections from the indwelling Ego to the outermost of its vehicles; while the effect of the recognition of these great truths upon the individuality that has for a time put off its robe of flesh, opens out a subject of paramount interest. Thus it is that on every plane Christ is the Fulfilling of the Law, and that "Salvation" is not a silly shiboleth but the logical and vital process of our advance into the unfoldment of the next stage of the limitless capacities of our being. Of these things I hope to write in another volume, should it be permitted to me, and in the meanwhile I would commend the present abstract statement of principles to the reader's attention in the hope that it may throw some light on the fundamental nature of these momentous questions. The great thing to bear in mind is that if a thing is true at all there must be a reason why it is true, and when we come to see this reason we know the truth at first hand for ourselves and not from some one else's report—then it becomes really our own and we begin to learn how to use it. This is the secret of the individual's progress in any art, science, or business, and the same method will serve equally well in our search after Life itself, and as we thus follow up the great quest we shall find that on every plane the Way, the Truth, and the Life are *One*.

"A little philosophy inclineth a man's mind to atheism, but depth in philosophy bringeth men's minds about to religion."—*Bacon. Essay xvi .*

THE DIVINE OFFERING

I take the present opportunity of a new edition to add a few pages on certain points which appear to me of vital importance, and the connection of which with the preceding chapters will, I hope, become evident as the reader proceeds. Assuming the existence in each individual of a creative power of thought which, in relation to himself, reflects the same power existing in the Universal Mind, our right employment of this power becomes a matter of extreme moment to ourselves. Its inverted use necessarily holds us fast in the bondage from which we are seeking to escape, and equally necessarily its right use brings us into Liberty; and therefore if any Divine revelation exists at all its purpose must be to lead us away from the inverted use of our creative faculty and into such a higher specializing of it as will produce the desired result. Now the purpose of the Bible is to do this, and it seeks to effect this work by a dual operation. It places before us that Divine Ideal of which I have already spoken, and at the same time bases this ideal upon the recognition of a Divine Sacrifice. These two conceptions are so intimately interwoven in Scripture that they cannot be separated, but at the present day there *is* a growing tendency to attempt to make this separation and to discard the conception of a Divine Sacrifice as unphilosophical, that is as having no nexus of cause and effect. What I want, therefore, to point out in these additional pages is that there is such a nexus, and that so far from being without a sequence of cause and effect it has its root in the innermost principles of our own being. It is not contrary to Law but proceeds from the very nature of the Law itself.

The current objection to the Bible teaching on this subject is that no such sacrifice could have been required by God, either because the Originating Energy can have no consciousness of Personality and is only a blind force, or because, if "God is Love," He could not demand such a sacrifice. On the former hypothesis we are of course away from the Bible teaching altogether and have nothing to do with it; but, as I have said elsewhere, the fact of our own consciousness of personality can only be accounted for by the existence, however hidden, of a corresponding quality in the Originating Spirit. Therefore I will confine my remarks to the question how Love, as the originating impulse of all creation, can demand such a sacrifice. And to my mind the answer is that God does not demand it. It is Man who demands it. It is the instinctive craving of the human soul for *certainty* that requires a demonstration so convincing as to leave no room for doubt of our perfectly happy relation to the Supreme Spirit, and consequently to all that flows from it, whether on the side of the visible or of the invisible. When we grasp the fact that such a standpoint of certainty is the necessary foundation for the building up in ourselves of the Divine Ideal then it becomes clear that to afford us this firm basis is the greatest work that the Spirit, in its relation to human personality, could do.

We are often told that the offering of sacrifices had its origin in primitive man's conception of his gods as beings which required to be propitiated so as to induce them to do good or abstain from doing harm; and very likely this was the case. The truth at the back of this conception is the feeling that there is a higher power upon which man is dependent; and the error is in supposing that this power is limited by an individuality which can be enriched by selling its good offices, or which blackmails you by threats. In either case it wants to get something out of you, and from this it follows that its own power of supplying its own wants must be limited, otherwise it would not require to be kept in good temper by gifts. In very undeveloped minds such a conception results in the idea of numerous gods, each having, so to say, his own particular line of business; and the furthest advance this mode of thought is capable of is the reduction of these various deities to two antagonistic powers of Good and of Evil. But the result in either case is the same, so long as we start with the hypothesis that the Good will do us more good and the Evil do us less harm by reason of our sacrifices, for then it logically follows that the more valuable your sacrifices and the oftener they are presented the better chance you have of good luck. Doubtless some such conception as this was held by the mass of the Hebrew people under the sacrificial system of the Levitical Law, and perhaps this was one reason why they were so prone to fall into idolatry—for in this view their fundamental notion was practically identical in its nature with that of the heathen around them. Of course this was not the fundamental idea embodied in the Levitical system itself. The root of that system was the symbolizing of a supreme ideal of reconciliation hereafter to be manifested in action. Now a symbol is not the thing symbolized. The purpose of a symbol is twofold, to put us upon enquiry as to the reality which it indicates, and to bring that reality to our minds by suggestion when we look at the symbol; but if it does not do this, and we rest only in the symbol, nothing will come of it, and we are left just where we were. That the symbolic nature of the Levitical sacrifice was clearly perceived by the deeper thinkers among the Hebrews is attested by many passages in the Bible—"Sacrifice and burnt offering thou wouldest not" (Psalms xl: 6, and li: 16) and other similar utterances; and the distinction between these symbols and that which they symbolized is brought out in the Epistle to the Hebrews by the argument that if those sacrifices had afforded a sufficient standpoint for the effectual realization of cleansing then the worshiper would not need to have repeated them because he would have no more consciousness of sin (Hebrews x: 2).

This brings us to the essential point of the whole matter. What we want is the certainty that there is no longer any separation between us and the Divine Spirit by reason of sin, either as overt acts of wrong doing or as error of principle; and the whole purpose of the Bible is to lead us to this assurance. Now such an assurance cannot be based on any sort of sacrifices that require repetition, for then we could never know whether we had given enough either in quality or quantity. It must be a once-for-all business or it is no use at all; and so the Bible makes the once-for-allness of the offering the essential point of its teaching. "He that has been bathed does not need to be bathed again" (John xiii: 10). "There is now no condemnation to them which are in Christ Jesus" (Romans viii: i).

Various intellectual difficulties, however, hinder many people from seeing the working of the law of cause and effect in this presentment. One is the question, How can moral guilt be transferred from one person to another? What is called the "forensic" argument (i.e., the court of law argument) that Christ undertook to suffer in our stead as our *surety* is undoubtedly open to this objection. Suretyship must by its very nature be confined to civil obligations and cannot be extended to criminal liability, and so the "forensic" argument may be set aside as very much a legal fiction. But if we realize the Bible teaching that Christ is the Son of God, that is, the Divine Principle of Humanity out of which we originated and subsisting in us all, however unconsciously to ourselves, then we see that sinners as well as saints are included in this Principle; and consequently that the Self-offering of Christ must actually include the self-offering of every human being in the acknowledgment (however unknown to his *objective* mentality) of his sin. If we can grasp this somewhat abstract point of view it follows that in the Person of Christ every human being, past, present, and to come, was self-offered for the condemnation of his sin—a *self* - condemnation and a *self* -offering, and hence a cleansing, for the simple reason that if you can get a man to realize his past error, really see his mistake, he won't do it again; and it is the perpetuation of sin and error that has to be got rid of—to do this universally would be to regain Paradise. Seen therefore in this light there is no question of transference of moral guilt, and I take it this is St. Paul's meaning when he speaks of our being partakers in Christ's death.

Then there is the objection, How can past sins be done away with? If we accept the philosophical conclusion that Time has no substantive existence then all that remains is states of consciousness. As I have said in the earlier part of this book, the Self-Contemplation of Spirit is the cause of all our perception of existence and environment; and consequently if the Self-Contemplation of the Spirit from any center of individualization is that of entire harmony and the absence of anything that would cause any consciousness of separation, then past sins cease to have any part in this self-recognition, and consequently cease to have any place in the world of existence. The foundation of the whole creative process is the calling into Light out of Darkness—"that which makes manifest is light"—and consequently the converse action is that of sending out of Light into Darkness, that is, into Notbeing. Now this is exactly what the Spirit says in the Bible—"I, even I, am He that blotteth out thy transgressions" (Isaiah xliii: 25). Blotting out is the sending out of manifestation into the darkness of non-manifestation, out of Being into Not-being; and in this way the past error ceases to have any existence and so ceases to have any further effect upon us. It is "blotted out," and from this new standpoint has never been at all; so that to continue to contemplate it is to give a false sense of existence to that which in effect has no existence. It is that Affirmation of Negation which is the root of all evil. It is the inversion of our God-given creative power of thought, calling into existence that which in the Perfect Life of the Spirit never had or could have any existence, and therefore it creates the sense of inharmony, opposition, and separation. Of course this is only relatively to ourselves, for we cannot create eternal principles. They are the Being of God; and as I have already shown these great Principles of the Affirmative may be summed up in the two words Love and Beauty—Love in essence and Beauty in manifestation; but since we can only live from the standpoint of our own consciousness we can make a false creation built upon the idea of opposites to the all-creating Love and Beauty, which false creation with all its accompaniments of limitation, sin, sorrow, sickness, and death, must necessarily be real to us until we perceive that these things were not created by God, the Spirit of the Affirmative, but by our own inversion of our true relation to the All-creating Being.

When, then, we view the matter in this light the Offering once for all of the Divine Sacrifice for the sin of the whole world is seen not to be a mere ecclesiastical dogma having no relation of cause and effect, but to be the highest application of the same principle of cause and effect by which the whole creation, ourselves included, has been brought into existence— the Self-Contemplation of Spirit producing corresponding manifestation, only now working on the level of Individual Personality.

As I have shown at the beginning of this book the cosmic manifestation of principles is not sufficient to bring out all that there is in them. To do this their action must be specialized by the introduction of the Personal Factor. They are represented by the Pillar Jachin, but it must be equilibrated by the Pillar Boaz, Law and Personality the two Pillars of the Universe; and in the One Offering we have the supreme combination of these two principles, the highest specialization of Law by the highest power of Personality. These are eternal principles, and therefore we are told that the Lamb was slain from the foundation of the world; and because "thoughts are things" this supreme manifestation of the creative interaction of Law and Personality was bound eventually to be manifested in concrete action in the world conditioned by time and space; and so it was that the supreme manifestation of the Love of God to meet the supreme need of Man took place. The history of the Jewish nation is the history of the working of the law of cause and effect, under the guidance of the Divine Wisdom, so as to provide the necessary conditions for the greatest event in the world's history; for if Christ was to appear it must be in *some* nation, in *some* place, and at *some* time: but to trace the steps by which, through an intelligible sequence of causes, these necessary conditions were provided belongs rather to an investigation of Bible history than to our present purpose, so I will not enter into these details here. But what I hope I have in some measure made clear is that there is a reason why Christ should be manifested, and should suffer, and rise again, and that so far from being a baseless superstition the Reconciling of the world to God through the One Offering once-for-all offered for the sin of the whole world, lays the immovable foundation upon which we may build securely for all the illimitable future.

OURSELVES IN THE DIVINE OFFERING

If we have grasped the principle I have endeavored to state in the last chapter we shall find that with this new standpoint a new life and a new world begin to open out to us. This is because we are now living from a new recognition of ourselves and of God. Eternal Truth, that which is the essential reality of Being, is *always* the same; it has never altered, for whatever is capable of passing away and giving place to something else is not eternal, and therefore the real essence of our being, as proceeding from God and subsisting in Him has always been the same. But this is the very fact which we have hitherto lost sight of; and since our perception of life is the measure of our individual consciousness of it, we have imposed upon ourselves a world of limitation, a world filled with the power of the negative, because we have viewed things from that standpoint. What takes place, therefore, when we realize the truth of our Redemption is not a change in our essential relation to the Parent Spirit, the Eternal Father, but an awakening to the perception of this eternal and absolutely perfect relation. We see that in reality it has never been otherwise for the simple reason that in the very nature of Being it *could* not be otherwise; and when we see this we see also that what has hitherto been wrong has not been the working of "the Father" but our conception of the existence of some other power, a power of negation, limitation, and destructiveness, the very opposite to all that the Creative Spirit, by the very fact of Its Creativeness, must be. That wonderful parable of the Prodigal Son shows us that he never ceased to be a son. It was not his Father who sent him away from home but his notion that he could do better "on his own," and we all know what came of it. But when he returned to the Father he found that from the Father's point of view he had never been otherwise than a son, and that all the trouble he had gone through was not "of the Father" but was the result of his own failure to realize what the Father and the Home really were.[9]

Now this is exactly the case with ourselves. When we wake up to the truth we find that, so far as the Father is concerned, we have always been in Him and in His home, for we are made in His image and likeness and are reflections of His own Being. He says to us "Son, thou art ever with me and all that I have is thine." The Self-Contemplation of Spirit is the Creative Power creating an environment corresponding to the mode of consciousness contemplated, and therefore in proportion as we contemplate ourselves as centers of individualization for the Divine Spirit we find ourselves surrounded by a new environment reflecting the harmonious conditions which preexist in the Thought of the Spirit.

This, then, is the sequence of Cause and Effect involved in the teaching of the Bible. Man is *in essence* a spiritual being, the reflection on the plane of individual personality of that which the All-Originating Spirit is in

Itself, and is thus in that reciprocal relation to the Spirit which is Love. This is the first statement of his creation in Genesis—God saw all that He had made and behold it was very good, Man included. Then the Fall is the failure of the lower mentality to realize that God IS Love, in a word that Love is the only ultimate Motive Power it is possible to conceive, and that the creations of Love cannot be otherwise than good and beautiful. The lower mentality conceives an opposite quality of Evil and thus produces a motive power the opposite of Love, which is Fear; and so Fear is born into the world giving rise to the whole brood of evil, anger, hatred, envy, lies, violence, and the like, and on the external plane giving rise to discordant vibrations which are the root of physical ill. If we analyze our motives we shall find that they are always some mode either of Love or Fear; and fear has its root in the recognition of some power other than Perfect Love, which is God the *One* all-embracing Good. Fear has a creative force which invertedly mimics that of Love; but the difference between them is that Love is eternal and Fear is not. Love as the Original Creative Motive is the only logical conclusion we can come to as to why we ourselves or any other creation exists. Fear is illogical because to regard it as having any place in the Original Creative Motive involves a contradiction in terms.

By accepting the notion of a dual power, that of Good *and* Evil, the inverted creative working of Fear is introduced with all its attendant train of evil things. This is the eating of the deadly tree which occasions the Fall, and therefore the Redemption which requires to be accomplished is a redemption from Fear—not merely from this or that particular fear but from the very Root of Fear, which root is unbelief in the Love of God, the refusal to believe that Love alone is the Creating Power in all things, whether small beyond our recognition or great beyond our conception. Therefore to bring about this Redemption there must be such a manifestation of the Divine Love to Man as, when rightly apprehended, will leave no ground for fear; and when we see that the Sacrifice of the Cross was the Self-Offering of Love made in order to provide this manifestation, then we see that all the links in the chain of Cause and Effect are complete, and that Fear never had any place in the Creative Principle, whether as acting in the creation of a world or of a man. The root, therefore, of all the trouble of the world consists in the Affirmation of Negation, in using our creative power of thought invertedly, and thus giving substance to that which *as principle* has no existence. So long as this negative action of thought continues so long will it produce its natural effect; whether in the individual or in the mass. The experience is perfectly real while it lasts. Its unreality consists in the fact that there was never any real need for it; and the more we grasp the truth of the all-embracingness of the *one* Good, both as Cause and as Effect, on all planes, the more the experience of its opposite will cease to have any place in our lives.

This truly New Thought puts us in an entirely new relation to the whole of our environment, opening out possibilities hitherto undreamt of, and this by an orderly sequence of law which is naturally involved in our new mental attitude; but before considering the prospect thus offered it is well to be quite clear as to what this new mental attitude really is; for it is our adoption of this attitude that is the Key to the whole position. Put briefly it is ceasing to include the idea of limitations in our conception of the working of the All-Creating Spirit. Here are some specimens of the way in which we limit the creative working of the Spirit. We say, I am too old now to start this or that new sort of work. This is to deny the power of the Spirit to vivify our physical or mental faculties, which is illogical if we consider that it is the same Spirit that brought us into any existence at all. It is like saying that when a lamp is beginning to burn low the same person who first filled it with oil cannot replenish it and make it burn brightly again. Or we say, I cannot do so and so because I have not the means. When you were fourteen did you know where all the means were coming from which were going to support you till now when you are perhaps forty or fifty? So you should argue that the same power that has worked in the past can continue to work in the future. If you say the means came in the past quite naturally through ordinary channels, that is no objection; on the contrary the more reason for saying that suitable channels will open in the future. Do you expect God to put cash into your desk by a conjuring trick? Means come through recognizable channels, that is to say we recognize the channels by the fact of the stream flowing through them; and one of our most common mistakes is in thinking that we ourselves have to fix the particular channel beforehand. We say in effect that the Spirit cannot open other channels, and so we stop them up. Or we say, our past experience speaks to the contrary, thus assuming that our past experiences have included all possibilities and have exhausted the laws of the universe, an assumption which is negatived by every fresh discovery even in physical science. And so we go on limiting the power of the Spirit in a hundred different ways.

But careful consideration will show that, though the modes in which we limit it are as numerous as the circumstances with which we have to deal, the thing with which we limit it is always the same—it is by the introduction of our own personality. This may appear at first a direct contradiction of all that I have said about the necessity for the Personal Factor, but it is not. Here is a paradox.

To open out into manifestation the wonderful possibilities hidden in the Creative Power of the Universe we require to do two things—to see that we ourselves are necessary as centers for focussing that power, and at the same time to withdraw the thought of ourselves as contributing anything to its efficiency. It is not I that work but the Power; yet the Power needs me because it cannot specialize itself without me—in a word each is the complementary of the other: and the higher the degree of specialization is to be the more necessary is the intelligent and willing co-operation of the individual.

This is the Scriptural paradox that "the son can do nothing of himself," and yet we are told to be "fellow-workers with God." It ceases to be a paradox, however, when we realize the relation between the two factors concerned, God and Man. Our mistake is in not discriminating between their respective functions, and putting Man in the place of God. In our everyday life we do this by measuring the power of God by our past experiences and the deductions we draw from them; but there is another way of putting Man in the place of God, and that is by the misconception that the All-Originating Spirit is merely a cosmic force without intelligence, and that Man has to originate the intelligence without which no specific purpose can be conceived. This latter is the error of much of the present day philosophy and has to be specially guarded against. This was perceived by some of the medieval students of these things, and they accordingly distinguished between what they called Animus Dei and Anima Mundi, the Divine Spirit and the Soul of the Universe. Now the distinction is this, that the essential quality of Animus Dei is Personality—not A Person, but the very Principle of Personality itself—while the essential quality of Anima Mundi is Impersonality. Then right here comes in that importance of the Personal Factor of which I have already spoken. The powers latent in the Impersonal are brought out to their fullest development by the operation of the Personal. This of course does not consist in changing the nature of those powers, for that is impossible, but in making such combinations of them by Personal Selection as to produce results which could not otherwise be obtained. Thus, for example, Number is in itself impersonal and no one can alter the laws which are inherent in it; but what we can do is to select particular numbers and the sort of relation, such as subtraction, multiplication, etc., which we will establish between them; and then by the inherent Law of Number a certain result is bound to work out. Now our own essential quality is the consciousness of Personality; and as we grow into the recognition of the fact that the Impersonal is, as it were, crying out for the operation upon it of the Personal in order to bring its latent powers into working, we shall see how limitless is the field that thus opens before us.

The prospect is wonderful beyond our present conception, and full of increasing glory if we realize the true foundation on which it rests. But herein lies the danger. It consists in not realizing that the Infinite of the Impersonal *is* and also that the Infinite of the Personal *is* . Both are Infinite and so require differentiation through our own personality, but in their essential quality each is the exact balance of the other—not in contradiction to each other, but as complementary to one another, each supplying what the other needs for its full expression, so that the two together make a perfect whole. If, however, we see this relation and our own position as the connecting link between them, we shall see only ourselves as the Personal Factor; but the more we realize, both by theory and experience, the power of human personality brought into contact with the Impersonal Soul of Nature, and employed with a Knowledge of its power and a corresponding exercise of the will, the less we shall be inclined to regard ourselves as the supreme factor in the chain of cause and effect Consideration of this argument points to the danger of much of the present day teaching regarding the exercise of Thought Power as a creative agency. The principle on which this teaching is based is sound and legitimate for it is inherent in the nature of things; but the error is in supposing that we ourselves are the ultimate source of Personality instead of merely the distributors and specializers of it. The logical result of such a mental attitude is that putting ourselves in the place of all that is worshiped as God which is spoken of in the second chapter of the Second Epistle to the Thessalonians and other parts of Scripture. By the very hypothesis of the case we then know no higher will than our own, and so are without any Unifying Principle to prevent the conflict of wills which must then arise—a conflict which must become more and more destructive the greater the power possessed by the contending parties, and which, if there were no counterbalancing power, must result in the ultimate destruction of the existing race of men.

But there is a counterbalancing power. It is the very same power used affirmatively instead of negatively. It is the power of the Personal with the Impersonal when used under the guidance of that Unifying Principle which the recognition of the *One*-ness of the Personal Quality in the Divine Spirit supplies. Those who are using the creative power of thought only from the standpoint of individual personality, have obviously less power than those who are using it from the standpoint of the Personality inherent in the Living Spirit which is the Source and Fountain of all energy and substance, and therefore in the end the victory must remain with these latter. And because the power by which they conquer is that of the Unifying Personality itself their victory must result in the establishment of Peace and Happiness throughout the world, and is not a power of domination but of helpfulness and enlightenment. The choice is between these two mottoes:— "Each for himself and Devil take the hindmost," or "God for us all." In proportion, therefore, as we realize the immense forces dormant in the Impersonal Soul of Nature, only awaiting the introduction of the Personal Factor to wake them up into activity and direct them to specific purposes, the wider we shall find the scope of the powers within the reach of man; and the more clearly we perceive the Impersonalness of the very Principle of Personality itself, the clearer our own proper position as affording the Differentiating Medium between these two Infinitudes will become to us.

The Impersonalness of the Principle of Personality looks like a contradiction in terms, but it is not. I combine these two seemingly contradictory terms as the best way to convey to the reader the idea of the essential Quality of Personality not yet differentiated into individual centers of consciousness for the doing of particular work. Looked at in this way the Infinite of Personality must have Unity of Purpose for its foundation, for otherwise it would consist of conflicting personalities, in which case we have not yet reached the *One* all-originating cause. Or to put it in another way, an Infinite Personality divided against itself would be an Infinite Insanity, a creator of a cosmic Bedlam which, as a scientific fact, would be impossible of existence. Therefore the conception of an Infinite of Personality necessarily implies a perpetual Unity of Purpose; and for the same reason this Purpose can only be the fuller and fuller expression of an Infinite Unity of Consciousness; and Unity of Consciousness necessarily implies the entire absence of all that would impair it, and therefore its expression can only be as Universal Harmony. If, then, the individual realizes this true nature of the source from which his own consciousness of personality is derived his ideas and work will be based upon this foundation, with the result that as between ourselves peace and good will towards men must accompany this mode of thought, and as between us and the strictly Impersonal Soul of Nature our increasing knowledge in that direction would mean increasing power for carrying out our principle of peace and good will. As this perception of our relation to the Spirit of God and the Soul of Nature spreads from individual to individual so the Kingdom of God will grow, and its universal recognition would be the establishing of the Kingdom of Heaven on earth.

Perhaps the reader will ask why I say the Soul of Nature instead of saying the material universe. The reason is that in using our creative power of Thought we do not operate directly upon material elements—to do that is the work of construction from without and not of creation from within. The whole tendency of modern physical science is to reduce all matter in the final analysis to energy working in a primary ether. Whence this energy and this ether proceed is not the subject of physical analysis. That is a question which cannot be answered by means of the vacuum tube or the spectroscope. Physical science is doing its legitimate work in pushing further and further back the unanalyzable residuum of Nature, but, however far back, an ultimate unanalyzable residuum there must always be; and when physical science brings us to this point it hands us over to the guidance of psychological investigation just as in the Divina Commedia Virgil transfers Dante to the guidance of Beatrice for the study of the higher realms. Various rates of rapidity of motion in this primary ether, producing various numerical combinations of positively and negatively electrified particles, result in the formation of what we know as the different chemical elements, and thus explains the phenomena of their combining quantities, the law by which they join together to form new substances only in certain exact numerical ratios. From the first movement in the primary ether to solid substances, such as wood or iron or our own flesh, is thus a series of vibrations in a succession of mediums, each denser than the preceding one out of which it was concreted and from which it receives the vibratory impulse. This is in effect what physical science has to tell us. But to get further back we must look into the world of the invisible, and it is here that psychological study comes to our aid. We cannot, however, study the invisible side of Nature by working from the outside and so at this point of our studies we find the use of the time-honored teaching regarding the parallelism between the Macrocosm and the Microcosm. If the Microcosm is the reproduction in ourselves of the same principles as exist in the Macrocosm or universe in which we have our being, then by investigating ourselves we shall learn the nature of the corresponding invisible principles in our environment. Here, then, is the application of the dictum of the ancient philosophy, "Know Thyself." It means that the only place where we can study the principles of the invisible side of Nature is in ourselves; and when we know them there we can transfer them to the larger world around us.

In the concluding chapters of my "Edinburgh Lectures on Mental Science" I have outlined the way in which the soul or mind operates upon the physical instrument of its expression, and it resolves itself into this—that the mental action inaugurates a series of vibrations in the etheric body which, in their turn, induce corresponding grosser vibrations in the molecular substance until finally mechanical action is produced on the outside. Now transferring this idea to Nature as a whole we shall see that if our mental action is to affect it in any way it can only be by the response of something at the back of material substance analogous to mind in ourselves; and that there is such a "something" interior to the merely material side of Nature is proved by what we may call the Law of Tendency, not only in animals and plants, but even in inorganic substances, as shown for instance in Professor Bose's work on the Response of Metals. The universal presence of this Law of Tendency therefore indicates the working of some non-material and, so to say, semi-intelligent power in the material world, a power which works perfectly accurately on its own lines so far as it goes, that is to say in a generic manner, but which does not possess that Personal power of *individual selection* which is necessary to bring out the infinite possibilities hidden in it. This is what is meant by the Soul of Nature, and it is for this reason I employ that term instead of saying the material universe. Which term to employ all depends on the mode of action we are contemplating. If it is construction from without, then we are dealing with the purely material universe. If we are seeking to bring about results by the exercise of our mental power from within, then we are dealing with the Soul of Nature. It is that control of the lower degree of intelligence by the higher of which I have spoken in my Edinburgh Lectures.

If we realize what I have endeavored to make clear in the earlier portion of this book, that the whole creation is produced by the operation of the Divine Will upon the Soul of Nature, it will be evident that we can set no limits to the potencies hidden in the latter and capable of being brought out by the operation of the Personal Factor upon it; therefore, granted a sufficiently powerful concentration of will, whether by an individual or a group of individuals, we can well imagine the production of stupendous effects by this agency, and in this way I would explain the statements made in Scripture regarding the marvelous powers to be exercised by the Anti-Christ, whether personal or collective. They are psychic powers, the power of the Soul of Man over the Soul of Nature. But the Soul of Nature is quite impersonal and therefore the moral quality of this action depends entirely on the human operator. This is the point of the Master's teaching regarding the destruction of the fig tree, and it is on this account He adds the warning as to the necessity for clearing our heart of any injurious feeling against others whenever we attempt to make use of this power (Mark xi: 20-26).

According to His teaching, then, this power of controlling the Soul of Nature by the addition of our own Personal Factor, however little we may be able to recognize it as yet, actually exists; its employment depends on our perception of the inner principles common to both, and it is for this reason the ancient wisdom was summed up in the aphorism "Know thyself." No doubt it is a wonderful Knowledge, but on analysis it will be found to be perfectly natural. It is the Knowledge of the cryptic forces of Nature. Now it is remarkable that this ancient maxim inscribed over the portals of the Temple of Delphi is not to be found in the Bible. The Bible maxim is not "Know thyself" but "Know the Lord." The great subject of Knowledge is not ourself but "the Lord"; and herein is the great difference between the two teachings. The one is limited by human personality, the other is based on the Infinitude of the Divine Personality; and because of this it includes human personality with all its powers over the Soul of Nature. It is a case of the greater including the less; and so the whole teaching of Scripture is directed to bringing us into the recognition of that Divine Personality which is the Great Original in whose image and likeness we are made. In proportion as we grow into the recognition of *this* our own personality will explain, and the creative power of our thought will cease to work invertedly until at last it will work only on the same principles of Life, Love and Liberty as the Divine Mind, and so all evil will disappear from our world. We shall not, as some systems teach, be absorbed into Deity to the extinction of our individual consciousness, but on the contrary our individual consciousness will continually expand, which is what St. Paul means when he speaks of our "increasing with the increase of God"—the continual expanding of the Divine element within us. But this can only take place by our recognition of ourselves as *receivers* of this Divine element. It is receiving into ourselves of the Divine Personality, a result not to be reached through human reasoning. We reason from premises which we have assumed, and the conclusion is already involved in the premises and can never extend beyond them. But we can only select our premises from among things that we know by experience, whether mental or physical, and accordingly our reasoning is always merely a new placing of the old things. But the receiving of the Divine Personality into ourselves is an entirely New Thing, and so cannot be reached by reasoning from old things. Hence if this Divine ultimate of the Creative Process is to be attained it must be by the Revelation of a New Thing which will afford a new starting-point for our thought, and this New Starting-point is given in the Promise of "the Seed of the Woman" with which the Bible opens. Thenceforward this Promise became the central germinating thought of those who based themselves upon it, thus constituting them a special race, until at last when the necessary conditions had matured the Promised Seed appeared in Him of whom it is written that He is the express image of God's Person (Heb. I: 3)—that is, the Expression of that Infinite Divine Personality of which I have spoken. "No man hath seen God at any time or can see Him," for the simple reason that Infinitude cannot be the subject of vision. To become visible there must be Individualization, and therefore when Philip said "Show us the Father," Jesus replied, "He that hath seen me hath seen the Father." The Word must become flesh before St. John could say, "That which was from the beginning, which we have heard, which we have seen with our eyes, which we have looked upon, and our hands have handled, of the Word of Life." This is the New Starting-point for the true New Thought—the New Adam of the New Race, each of whom is a new center for the working of the Divine Spirit. This is what Jesus meant when he said, "Except ye eat the flesh and drink the blood of the Son of Man ye have no life in you. My flesh is meat indeed, and my blood is drink indeed—" such a contemplation of the Divine Personality in Him as will cause a like receiving of the Divine Personality into individualization in ourselves—this is the great purpose of the Creative Process in the individual. It terminates the old series which began with birth after the flesh and inaugurates a New Series by birth after the Spirit, a New Life of infinite unfoldment with glorious possibilities beyond our highest conception.

But all this is logically based upon our recognition of the Personalness of God and of the relation of our individual personality to this Eternal and Infinite Personality, and the result of this is Worship—not an attempt to "butter up" the Almighty and get Him into good temper, but the reverent contemplation of what this Personality must be in Itself; and when we see it to be that Life, Love, Beauty, etc., of which I spoke at the beginning of this book we shall learn to love Him for what He IS, and our prayer will be "Give me more of Thyself." If we realize the great truth that the Kingdom of Heaven is *within* us, that it is the Kingdom of the innermost of our own being and of all creation, and if we realize that this innermost is the place of the Originating Power where Time and Space do not exist and therefore antecedent to all conditions, then we shall see the true meaning of Worship. It is the perception of the Innermost Spirit as eternally subsisting independently of all conditioned manifestation, so that in the true worship our consciousness is removed from the outer sphere of existence to the innermost center of unconditioned being. There we find the Eternal Being of God pure and simple, and we stand reverently in this Supreme Presence knowing that it is the Source of our own being, and wrapt in the contemplation of This, the conditioned is seen to flow out from It. Perceiving this the conditioned passes out of our consideration, for it is seen not to be the Eternal Reality—we have reached that level of consciousness where Time and Space remain no longer. Yet the reverence which the vision of this Supreme Center of all Being cannot fail to inspire is coupled with a sense of feeling quite at home with It. This is because as the Center of *all* Being it is the center of our own being also. It is one-with-ourselves. It is recognizing Itself from our own center of consciousness; so that here we have got back to that Self-contemplation of Spirit which is the first movement of the Creating Power, only now this Self-contemplation is the action of the All-Originating Spirit upon Itself from the center of our own consciousness. So this worship in the Temple of the Innermost is at once reverent adoration and familiar intercourse—not the familiarity that breeds contempt, but a familiarity producing Love, because as it increases we see more clearly the true Life of the Spirit as the continual interaction of Love and Beauty, and the Spirit's recognition of ourselves as an integral portion of Its own Life. This is not an unpractical dreamy speculation but has a very practical bearing. Death will some day cease to be, for the simple reason that Life alone can be the enduring principle; but we have not yet reached this point in our evolution. Whether any in this generation will reach it I cannot say; but for the rank and file of us the death of the body seems to be by far the more probable event. Now what must this passing out of the body mean to us? It must mean that we find ourselves without the physical vehicle which is the instrument through which our consciousness comes in touch with the external world and all the interests of our present daily life. But the mere putting off of the body does not of itself change the mental attitude; and so if our mind is entirely centered upon these passing interests and external conditions the loss of the instrument by which we held touch with them must involve a consciousness of desire for the only sort of life we have known coupled with a consciousness of our inability to participate in it, which can only result in a consciousness of distress and confusion such as in our present state we cannot imagine.

On the other hand if we have in this world realized the true principle of the Worship of the Eternal Source from which all conditioned life flows out—an inner communing with the Great Reality—we have already passed beyond that consciousness of life which is limited by Time and Space; and so when we put off this mortal body we shall find ourselves upon familiar ground, and therefore not wandering in confusion but quite at home, dwelling in the same light of the Eternal in which we have been accustomed to dwell as an atmosphere enveloping the conditioned life of to-day. Then finding ourselves thus at home on a plane where Time and Space do not exist there will be no question with us of duration. The consciousness will be simply that of peaceful, happy being. That a return to more active personal operation will eventually take place is evidenced by the fact that the basis of all further evolution is the differentiating of the Undifferentiated Life of the Spirit into specific channels of work, through the intermediary of individual personality without which the infinite potentialities of the Creative Law cannot be brought to light. Therefore, however various our opinions as to its precise form, Resurrection as a principle is a necessity of the creative process. But such a return to more active life will not mean a return to limitations, but the opening of a new life in which we shall transcend them all, because we have passed beyond the misconception that Time and Space are of the Essence of Life. When the misconception regarding Time and Space is entirely eradicated all other limitations must disappear because they have their root in this primary one—they are only particular forms of the general proposition. Therefore though Form with its accompanying relations of Time and Space is necessary for manifestation, these things will be found not to have any force in themselves thus creating limitation, but to be the reflection of the mode of thought which projects them as the expression of itself.

Nor is there any inherent reason why this process should be delayed till some far-off future. There is no reason why we should not commence at once. No doubt our inherited and personally engendered modes of thought make this difficult, and by the nature of the process it will be only when *all* our thoughts are conformed to this principle that the complete victory will be won. But there must be a commencement to everything, and the more we habituate ourselves to live in that Center of the Innermost where conditions do not exist, the more we shall find ourselves gaining control over outward conditions, because the stream of conditioned life flows out from the Center of Unconditioned Life, and therefore this intrinsic principle of Worship has in it the promise both of the life that now is and of that which is to come. Only we must remember that the really availing worship is that of the Undifferentiated Source *because It is the Source*, and not as a backhanded way of diverting the stream into some petty channel of conditions, for that would only be to get back to the old circle of limitation from which we are seeking to escape.

But if we realize these things we have already laid hold of the Principle of Resurrection, and in point of principle we are already living the resurrection life. What progress we may make in it depends on our practical application of the principle; but simply as principle there is nothing in the principle itself to prevent its complete working at any moment. This is why Jesus did not refer resurrection to some remote point of time but said, "I am the resurrection and the life." No principle can carry in itself an opposite and limiting principle contradictory of its own nature, and this is as true of the Principle of Life as of any other principle. It is we who by our thought introduce an opposite and limiting principle and so hinder the working of the principle we are seeking to bring into operation; but so far as the Principle of Life itself is concerned there is *in it* no reason why it should not come into perfect manifestation here and now.

This, then, is the true purpose of worship. It is to bring us into conscious and loving intercourse with the Supreme Source of our own being, and seeing this we shall not neglect the outward forms of worship. From what we now know they should mean more to us than to others and not less; and in especial if we realize the manifestation of the Divine Personality in Jesus Christ and its reproduction in Man, we shall not neglect His last command to partake of that sacred memorial to His flesh and blood which He bequeathed to His followers with the words "This do in remembrance of Me."

This holy rite is no superstitious human invention. There are many theories about it, and I do not wish to combat any of them, for in the end they all seem to me to bring us to the same point, that being cleansed from sin by the Divine Love we are now no longer separate from God but become "partakers of the Divine-Nature" (II Peter I: 4). This partaking of the Divine Nature could not be more accurately represented than by our partaking of bread and wine as symbols of the Divine Substance and the Divine Life, thus made emblematic of the whole Creative Process from its beginning in the Divine Thought to its completion in the manifestation of that Thought as Perfected Man; and so it brings vividly before us the remembrance of the Personality of God taking form as the Son of Man. We are all familiar with the saying that thoughts become things; and if we affirm the creative power of our own thought as reproducing itself in outward form, how much more must we affirm the same of that Divine Thought which brings the whole universe into existence; so that in accordance with our own principles the Divine Idea of Man was logically bound to show itself in the world of time and space as the Son of God and the Son of man, not two differing natures but one complete whole, thus summing up the foundation principle of all creation in one Undivided Consciousness of Personality. Thus "the Word" or Divine Thought of Man "became flesh," and our partaking of the symbolic elements keeps in our remembrance the supreme truth that this same "Word" or Thought of God in like manner takes form in ourselves as we open our own thought to receive it. And further, if we realize that throughout the universe there is only *One* Originating Life, sending forth only *One* Original Substance as the vehicle for its expression, then it logically follows that *in essence* the bread is a portion of the eternal Substance of God, and the wine a portion of the eternal Life of God. For though the wine is of course also a part of the Universal Substance, we must remember that the Universal Substance is itself a manifestation of the Life of the All-Creating Spirit, and therefore this fluid form of the primary substance has been selected as representing the eternal flowing of the Life of the Spirit into all creation, culminating in its supreme expression in the consciousness of those who, in the recognition of these truths, seek to bring their heart into union with the Divine Spirit. From such considerations as these it will be seen how vast a field of thought is covered by Christ's words "Do this in remembrance of Me."

In conclusion, therefore, do not let yourselves be led astray by any philosophy that denies the Personality of God. In the end it will be found to be a foolish philosophy. No other starting-point of creation is conceivable than the Self-Contemplation of the Divine Spirit, and the logical sequence from this brings us to the ultimate result of the Creative Process in the statement that "if any man be in Christ he is a New creature," or as the margin has it "a new creation" (II Cor. v: 17). Such vain philosophies have only one logical result which is to put *yourself* in the place of God, and then what have you to lean upon in the hour of trial? It is like trying to climb up a ladder that is resting against nothing. Therefore, says the Apostle Paul, "Beware lest any man spoil you through philosophy and vain deceit, after the tradition of man, after the rudiments of the world, and not after Christ." (Col. II: 8.) The teaching of the Bible is sound philosophy, sound reasoning, and sound science because it starts with the sound premises that all Creation proceeds out of God, and that Man is made in the image and likeness of his Creator. It nowhere departs from the Law of Cause and Effect, and by the orderly sequence of this law it brings us at last to the New Creation both in ourselves and in our environment, so that we find the completion of the Creative Process in the declaration "the tabernacle of God is with men" (Rev. xxi: 3), and in the promise "This is the Covenant that I will make with them after those days (i.e., the days of our imperfect apprehension of these things) saith the Lord, I will dwell *in them* , and walk in *them*, and I will be their God, and they shall be my people, and I will put my laws into their hearts, and in their minds will I write them, and their sins and their iniquities will I remember no more" (Heb. x: 16. II Cor. vi: 16. Jeremiah xxxi: 33).

Truly does Bacon say, "A little philosophy inclineth a man's mind to atheism, but depth in philosophy bringeth men's minds about to religion." —Bacon, Essay, xvi.

FOOTNOTES

Footnote 1: See my Doré Lectures, 1909.

Footnote 2: See my Edinburgh Lectures on Mental Science.

Footnote 3: See my Doré Lectures, 1909.

Footnote 4: For the relation between conscious and sub-conscious mind see my "Edinburgh Lectures on Mental Science."

Footnote 5: See "Self-Synthesis" by Dr. Cornwall Round.

Footnote 6: For the relation between subjective and objective mind see my "Edinburgh Lectures on Mental Science."

Footnote 7: This view, it may be remarked, is not necessarily incompatible with the conception of reincarnation, on which theory the final resurrection or transmutation of the body would terminate the series of successive lives and deaths, thus bringing the individual out of the circle of generation, which is the circle of Karma. I may, perhaps, have the opportunity of considering this subject on some future occasion.

Footnote 8: See my "Bible Mystery and Bible Meaning."

Footnote 9: See "Bible Mystery and Bible Meaning" by the present author.

Printed in the United States
143846LV00004B/16/A